Triple "e" Productions

Acknowledgments

A special thanks to the editorial focus group investing numerous hours reading through material and participating in discussions. Their input and recommendations contributed greatly in achieving clarity in delivering this information, and the integrity behind its introduction, to the mainstream. Many have extensive backgrounds in similar areas of investigation and are capable of offering Foundation Sketches, speaking to groups, etc.

Brad Stewart   W. Bradstreet Stewart is a specialist in ancient traditions of sacred knowledge with an emphasis in metaphysical cosmology. He is founder and director of the Sacred Science Institute (www.sacred science.com) and the Glass Bead Game (www.glassbeadgame.com), organizations created with the intent of disseminating scared knowledge from the great esoteric traditions of the past. The Sacred Science Institute is an Internet resource center containing an extensive collection of the rarest metaphysical and cosmological works. Based upon the development of this knowledge, the Glass Bead Game was created as an interactive experimental laboratory in multi-dimensional transformation. The Sacred Science Institute also offers services such as personality and life purpose analysis based upon an ancient, lost system of Vedic astrology.

Dan McGrath   B. S. B. A. Promotional Coordinator for Personal and Professional Development Organization. Currently pursuing a Masters Degree in Spiritual Psychology.

Debra A. Franco   A transformation specialist in the San Diego area. Her expertise in multi-dimensional healing is internationally recognized. Specializing in young children, adults and animal; "all bodies" subtle energy, i.e., ethnic, physical, mental, etc.

Christina Monterastelli A highly respected teacher, visionary and minister of metaphysics. She has professional experience that spans 40 years of research, education and healing.

G. Thomas Edwards Artist, author and graphic designer, he is responsible for the book's design, layout and visual appeal.

Eric Emanuel A special thanks for his devoted support and encouragement.

Lahny McCrae The candidate for developing a baseline of understanding. Informed, curious and committed to the development of the human potential; our ideal audience.

Harold Wirk Artist and caraciturist. Harrold provided all the artwork for body types.

David Morgan Many thanks for insightful advice, recommendations, and enthusiastic support.

Michael Cohen The key participant in initiating the first of several drafts. His encouragement and devotion to the information's value is responsible for its existence today. Without him, there would not have been the beginning as it was in this process: an organized compilation of thoughts, notes and teaching concepts that began The Elephant's Knee.

Zannah The editor and glue; a collaborative associate, author and key participant in facilitating the manifestation of the book. Her commitment and contributions to the big picture and willingness to endure the process are infinite.

For Foundation Sketches of family, friends or associates please contact Reel Promotions at 760-632-9694 or e-mail: *triple"e"@reelpromos.com*. If not in the immediate area of a specialist, sketches can often be facilitated through using a combination of phone interviews, photographs and/or a video presentation. Call For fees, guidelines and recommendations.

http://www.reelpromos.com

On The Elephant's Knee
A Triple "e" Productions Book

Publishing History
First printing June 1998

Publisher
Triple "e" Productions
P.O. Box 8790
South Lake Tahoe, CA 96158
e-mail: triple"e"@reelpromos.com

ISBN 1-889211-06-0

Printed in the United States of America

On The Elephant's Knee

"I have met very few men who are smarter than their own weaknesses".

Thomas M. Easley

An ancient parable describes a king's meditation on the nature of the elephant:

One day the king assembled all the blind men of the town, and told his servant: "Show these men an elephant."

The servant had one blind man touch the head of the elephant, another the ear, another the trunk, another the tusk, another a foot, another the back, another the tail, and another the tuft of the tail; and to each blind man he said, "you are touching the elephant."

The king asked the blind men: "What is the elephant like?"

The man who had touched the head said: "A pot." The one who had touched the ear said: " A fan." And so it went: the trunk became a plow; the tusk, a plowshare; the foot, a pillar; the back, a granary; the tail, a pestle; and the tuft of the tail, a broom.

Then they began to argue with each other, saying: "An elephant is like this – no, it is not, it is like this – I tell you it is not"; until in the end they came to blows.

... and the king enjoyed the scene very much.

Table Of Contents

Foreword

I met Thomas Easley at an Art Gallery in South Lake Tahoe, California in 1996. He had just returned from Europe and Asia where he had spent most of his adult life as a journalist, author, artist and teacher. Knowing this world is filled with great artists and authors and having interviewed a few as a journalist, I treated our initial encounter somewhat insignificantly. Twelve months later, I find it challenging in trying to convey the significance that this man brings to our world and the price that he has had to pay in making it available to the masses. His experience in delivering what was once regarded as a highly protected and sacred body of knowledge is laced with integrity and a sense of justice. One would not perceive this man to be the gatekeeper of such wealth of hidden knowledge. I have watched him in the company of those with power. The wisdom is rarely revealed and still he continues to guard it in many circles. This comes from his witnessing its abuse. It has taken many years to convince him that it's time and that we as human beings are mature enough to assess our own weaknesses; to identify the weakest link and try to make it stronger. In many ways he is just a man with frailties, a past of tragedy, of wonder and childish desires. In other ways, he is a voice that comes from the past; from a time when there was a unification of thought and understanding; where the desire to manipulate and control was non-existent; a time when mutual understanding and human potential were shared as a part of one's minimum daily requirement for a harmonious existence.

Thomas Easley was told, "If you take this information out-side, you will not go to heaven. It is not information for the masses". This was a rather severe direction to give to a young man. And so he followed this dictate until the knowledge itself would no longer allow him to tolerate these kinds of sugges-tions. He has spent the last thirty years teaching, sharing and assisting great minds in achieving clarity and power with the use of this vital wisdom. Often times he chose to retreat by seeking solitude in Europe and Asia. The wise yet simple mountain man went back and forth to India and Italy where he was revered as one of this world's finest artists...Italy's "Canaletto Nuevo." There he began to follow his own instincts; to use the knowledge to transform. "Knowledge is like having a lot of paper currency on a desert island. If you can't spend it, it becomes worthless." He decided it was time to take the knowledge to the masses where it could be utilized. Easley is hopeful it will be used to transform, to create harmonious work environments, to make a difference and to perpetuate the evolution of a species that has been "de-evolving" for 9,000 years. He cannot give all that he has stored in his capable mind but, in cooperation with many other leading metaphysicists and theorists, he can assist in bringing this exceptional insight into the hearts and minds of many. It is information everyone will recognize on some level because we all have received rem-nants of it from time to time. Many have delivered the infor-mation from a place of intuition. It may be a little misconstrued or not quite congruent with the integrity of the whole concept but, for the most part, good intentions prevail by provoking thought and initiating change for the betterment of mankind. It's time to untangle a few knots and smooth out a few wrin-kles...even On an Elephant's Knee.

This book is but a tiny part of a huge body of universal wis-dom. It is knowledge that is often thought to be as old as 30-60,000 years but, for all practical purposes, it can only be traced back 9,000 years. It is not information that any one person can own. This includes all scribes of knowledge, be they esoteric, religious, practical, new age or fundamental. Knowledge is a universal privilege and, how we decide to use it largely determines the direction we will take as an evolutionary species. Many have taken parts of this great understanding and delivered it in a way that served the needs of the masses of the time, hence religions were born and theories manifested. This presentation addresses only the Knee of the Elephant as opposed to the whole. It is a small but significant beginning in facilitating movement. The Knowledge has afforded a process called Foundation Sketching. This allows one to create a personal profile or sketch for themselves or others. It's a little like looking in a magnifying mirror. I have used it on many occasions and where I was once assumptive or judgmental, I often find myself employing understanding and tolerance. I now understand why I don't understand and that, with this knowledge, everyone can, and deserves to be, understood. It has granted me an opportunity to assess my environment and just enjoy being in it or not. I have thoroughly enjoyed doing sketches for others and find it very rewarding. These are valuable when trying to sort through relationship problems with a spouse or friend, or career issues. The information does not discriminate and can be used on kids, animals and a variety of environments. It has been useful in exploring ways to spend energy in an overactive child or adults with ADD, the discovery frequently eliminating the need for medication or incorporating a dietary requirement or restriction. It's not information that will ever harm anyone. It's very basic and merely offers a blueprint from which one can build upon. It's a start. We are uncovering something quite wonderful here... in a way that will not permit abuse, religious stigmas, or attack. Thomas Easley is very courageous and quite dedicated to making this one of his responsibilities in this life time. He and I have had many discussions with regards to the role of religious devotion, intervals, other laws, hydrogens and the ever growing understanding of multi-dimensional visual reasoning. In the interest of brevity and clarity, I can best summarize his interpretation by citing an excerpt from a letter he wrote to Dannion Brinkley in seeking his assessment. "Thus far I have learned what I believe to be one enduring lesson: That man is a multi-dimensional being who, as a result of spiritual predators and hereditary fears, is deprived of the wonder of a multi-dimensional perspective. This is our primary and most ancient error. On the Elephant's Knee, if it is successful, will help correct this error by coaxing a gradual and non-conflicting reassessment of our linear dimensional definition of "I". As I have understood it, "I", when it evolves from the subject of observation, no matter how personal or profound that subject, to the state of non-participating observation, becomes more certainly an image made in the image of God." Many wonderful people have brought their practical understanding to the table via editorial focus groups and publications in print. Thomas believes in verification. The process of verification increases clarity. This is why he seeks to verify. "You may not be able to verify something but, through the process of seeking verification, what is and is not true becomes more clear". This will offer some protection and maintain the integrity of processing knowledge. This is not a book about an experience. Everyone has an experience to share and each is significant in its own right. This book helps one get a little closer to that which initiates the experience. The parable of the blind men and the elephant serves to illustrate how incomplete our knowledge is; nothing is decided. As Easley said, "We must admit at least the possibility that everything we believe to be true is not true."

Zannah

Origins of Foundation Knowledge

Foundation Knowledge, as presented in this book, traces back to the work of G. I. Gurdjieff, a mystic, cosmologist, philosopher, born in 1866 in the Calladacian Greek quarter of Alezandropol on the Russian side of the Russo-Turkish border. Gurdjieff, as a young man, manifested a natural inclination towards spiritual philosophies. Having spent time in both Christian and Islamic monasteries, he was inspired to found an organization called the "Seekers of Truth," dedicated to unveiling the ancient esoteric traditions of the great civilizations of the past. In the course of their search for this ancient invaluable wisdom, Gurdjieff and his compatriots scoured the Middle and Eastern worlds from Egypt through Arabia, Persia, India, and Tibet for living schools or teachers of this ancient wisdom. Gurdjieff was fortunate enough to have traveled these regions at a time when living masters and traditions existed as they rarely do today, and privileged to have studied at such places as the Sarmoung Monastery in Tibet where he is purported to have had some of his most profound insights. By the year 1914, Gurdjieff had synthesized his twenty years of practice and research into a cohesive transformational and cosmological system known today as the "Fourth Way." (For complete information and bibliographies on Gurdjieff and the Fourth Way organizations, see *www.gurdjieff.org*)

The origins of this system as gleaned through Gurdjieff's extensive travels and studies are based upon the ancient perennial philosophies represented by the esoteric, scientific, and philosophical traditions. Gurdjieff was fortunate n his search to have been exposed to and initiated into a variety of ancient traditions, allowing him to recognize the inherent similarities and foundations upon which all esoteric traditions are based. The primary traditions to which Gurdjieff was exposed include Sufism (Islamic Mysticism), Orthodox Christianity, Hinduism, Buddhism, as well as traditions of magic and esoteric science existent since ancient times in Egypt, Persia and India.

The aspects and structure of Foundation Knowledge presented in this book show a direct correlation in form and terminology to specific representations of perennial, traditional knowledge in several of the above – mentioned traditions. For instance, in the category of body type, all characteristics are delimited according to their planetary characteristics (Sun, Moon, Mercury, Venus, Mars, Jupiter, Saturn) without regard for the additions of the "more recently discovered" planets (Uranus, Neptune, Pluto). This procedure is based upon the traditional (as seen in Vedic, Chaldean and Egyptian astrology) approach which sees the aggregate of the primary seven planets (including Sun and Moon as observed luminaries from the perspective of Earth) as an inherent aspect of Universal order, referred to by Gurdjieff as the Law of Seven.

The center of focus (intellectual, emotional, instinctual, and moving) which is determined through the system of analysis presented in The Elephant's Knee is correlative to what are know as the subtle bodies in traditional knowledge (roughly translated from various ancient traditions as the psychic or mental body, the astral or emotional body, the physical body, and the etheric body or more abstractly defined body).

The concepts presented as Alchemy in Foundation Knowledge are clearly identifiable as terminology stemming from ancient esoteric traditions intent on the analysis of the composition of the psycho-spiritual elements of the human being. Alchemy is the ancient science of recognition and combination of elements, both physical and psycho-spiritual, with the intention of the manipulation of the base elements into purer and more refined elements. Alchemy is the source and foundation of what is now modern chemistry (without the spiritual and psychological interpretations, of course, nor the more profound physical transmutative capabilities).

The category of Chief Feature is a bit harder to correlate with the traditional systems, mostly due to the fact that Chief Feature is of a lower order causative factor, unlike the other categories which represent a more primary order of causation. This means that Chief Feature is influenced more heavily by circumstance, environment, society and the like, compared to the other categories which are more cosmically predetermined. Besides this, Chief Feature, being a more superficial psychological phenomenon is, in most traditions, discussed in the introductory moral teachings and codes which form prerequisites for the more profound teaching which follow. Some examples of this are the Buddha's Noble Eight-Fold Path and Patanjali's Yoga Sutas which first direct the aspirant towards a moral purification overcoming the negative aspects of the ego, such as those represented in the Christian tradition as the seven deadly sins.

Lastly, Essence is the equivalent of what we, in the Western traditions, would call the soul, the essence, or core of our individualized personality. This is not to be confused with the concept of Spirit, absolute nature, Atman or Self, which in all perennial philosophies takes on a unified, all-pervasive element devoid of any superficial personality characteristics. Essence defines the core of our psychological being, who we are in this world, which defines our role and purpose on this planet, equivalent to dharma in the Indian, Vedic philosophy.

The analysis derived by *On The Elephant's Knee* is one based upon ancient fundamental principles of structure and form in the world of manifest reality. It simply reveals fundamental aspects of human personality based upon universal causative principles of order and correspondence, proven to be true by traditions which have survived for over 5,000 years. In a world of chaos and confusion, *On The Elephant's Knee* offers a system of understanding and insight which could, without exaggeration, transform the limited perspective of the common man into something similar to the perspective and vision of the sages of ancient times.

Bradstreet Stewart

Introduction

Seven years ago, Michael Cohen came to my studio with a tape recorder and began asking me questions about Foundation Knowledge. We talked, we paused, we took walks. The pages which follow reflect the tempo of our conversation and the hope we shared that something beneficial would develop from our exchange.

Have you ever wondered why you see things one way and your friends another? Wondered why you enjoy certain foods, clothes, music, actors, movies, activities, and people but have a deep antipathy toward others? Wondered why you get along so well with some people while others incite profound ire? Have you ever wondered why you enjoy specific sports, support particular politicians and causes, cherish certain friends, while your spouse, partner, sibling, child or parent has exactly opposite tastes? Have you considered why some people become lifelong friends and others simply blur into a vague landscape of migrating faces? Or why do two people fall in love, only to discover within months that they are incompatible?

The causes for our differences, behavioral preferences and tendencies are so complex and varied that a meaningful understanding is difficult to achieve. Yet, where do we turn to advance our understanding and by such advancement make a more unified whole of our often fragmented lives? There are so many conflicting religions, sects and cults, many of which offer valid, yet diverse, approaches to understanding the human condition. *On The Elephant's Knee* is, in a sense, just another part of the King's elephant, another approach, one which can be applied in tandem with all other studies, traditions and disciplines.

The basis upon which we have built *On The Elephant's Knee* are primarily fragments of an ancient body of knowledge called, for simplicitys sake, "Foundation Knowledge."

Foundation Knowledge serves as a partial standard upon which all other typing systems and practices are built. It illustrates the rule of often hidden laws which govern human existence beyond the influence of the four laws of physics. Many select organizations, politicians, spiritual leaders, healers and successful business moguls have a factual or intuitive possession of this knowledge. Until now, the acquisition of and application of Foundation Knowledge has been reserved primarily for an elite and chosen few who too often use the knowledge to fulfill selfish rather than objective goals.

Often considered impracticably mysterious, Foundation Knowledge is, in fact, exceedingly practical and can be verified and applied by anyone in a relatively short period of time.

Foundation Knowledge can be seen as a light, an integrator that adds direction and clarity, a binding force that unites in understanding many of those observations made by us which we have not previously been able to recall and process. We lose nothing by adding this Knowledge to our current understanding of religion, life and the human condition. It poses no threat to any other doctrines or systems. All of the knowledge categories within *On The Elephant's Knee* are verifiable. Throughout history, numerous societies be they religious or scientific have harbored this knowledge and used it to assess prevailing movements and to perpetuate growth and dominance over the less informed. It is necessary, we believe, for all people to have access to Foundation Knowledge. To evolve as a species both the field and the seed, the whole and the part, must be equally fertile and equally capable of actualizing their full potential. By integrating rather then isolating knowledge systems the mystery and intrigue of deified elitism is dispelled, the power and manipulative potential of cunning minds diminished, and the road to a greater understanding of what is ultimately possible as a species is made more accessible.

This book, *On The Elephant's Knee*, stands as a snapshot, a small part of a greater body of knowledge.

Have you ever wondered how the pyramids were built? Did they remove gravity from the stones? Imagine possessing knowledge that would allow you to reconstruct gravity, to reconstruct electromagnetism. Would you like to remain aware of multiple truths without becoming contradictory, to see as the laws see, to create within yourself an identity capable of coexisting simultaneously in more than one dimension? Would you like to live in a world without strangers, know others intimately when meeting them for the first time? Would you like to gain more control, to know your weaknesses as intimately as those who would use "mind control" against you know them? Would you like a better shield, more strength to protect yourself and those you love from being manipulated? Would you like to better identify a predatory charlatan before he overcomes your will and resources?

According to Foundation Knowledge, all of human behavior is influenced in part by at least five principles, or laws, which create specific tendencies. These tendencies arise in people at conception and significantly prejudice our subsequent behavior. Once we know these tendencies, choices which presently elude us are made available and we are granted an additional possibility of understanding. And this "new" understanding renders more objective our attitude towards processing the behavior of ours and other people. It also enables us to predict the likely outcome of such behavior. Foundation Knowledge provides keys to unlock many of the mysteries of ordinary life: why one man loves the stench of exercise and another hates it, why we just "end up" in a particular city, in a particular job and in a particular circle, why we or someone we like (or dislike) has particular attitudes toward:

Food and Diet
Clothes and Cleanliness
Sex
Romance
Job
House, Car, Neighborhood, the Environment
Politics
Punishment

Foundation Knowledge helps to predict, with surprising accuracy, these preferences and predilections. By reading this book, by attempting to locate and observe your type, alchemy, chief feature, and center of focus, you will learn how to better harmonize your interactions with your boss, family and friends, how to pursue romantic partners that make sense for you, find jobs that suit your overall being, establish friendships that contribute to your overall happiness.

The five foundation principles or laws are referred to as: (1) body type, (2) alchemy, (3) chief feature, (4) center of focus and (5) essence. Generally, to discover and determine one's predominate principles, or those of another person, one should first try to be aware of what is most obvious about the person (for example: is the person active or passive, optimistic or pessimistic, a Martial type or a Venusian type, and so on). Then one should next consider what is the second most obvious characteristic (such as, is the person's chief feature destructiveness or power, or fear, etc.). Once these characteristics have been isolated then a third principle needs to be targeted (is the person's alchemy gold or lead), the fourth most obvious, (determining center of focus: emotional, intellectual, instinctive, etc.) and then the fifth (essence) would be the final observation. When taken as a whole, and allowing for the fact that Foundation Knowledge is alive, the five principles provide a comprehensive measure (70 to 80% accuracy) of where we are and where we can go, of how limiting or conducive our weaknesses and strengths are. Almost any behavior can be better understood and influenced by utilizing an application of the Five Principles.

Each chapter in this book provides a comprehensive analysis of individual principles demonstrating practical effects on people's personalities and preferences. To best illustrate and facilitate a processing of this information we analyze movie stars, athletes, politicians and other public figures; showing body type, alchemy, chief feature and focal center in action. It's important to snapshot or sketch a person, to align them with objective standards (i.e., why a person typically likes and dislikes other people and how he would be expected to respond to ordinary life as identified by Foundation Knowledge). Our analysis, however, is only a draft of Foundation Knowledge at work, a "Foundation Sketch," but once you understand the concepts, you will have a baseline that will provide a number of tools to use in arriving at your own conclusions. At a glance when you first meet someone you will know much more then their name and nationality. You will know the prejudices and preferences of their body type, alchemy, chief feature, center of focus, and how the likely interactions of these tendencies with your own will play out. We start with sketches: a rough attempt to apply Foundation Knowledge to our observations, then work toward greater accuracy. With time, our percentage ratio improves.

We've said that the principles are maps, sign posts, to our

behavior. We present them separately as five distinct para-
meters of human interaction although, in reality, they
operate as sentient interlocking levers. In a personality like
Arnold Schwarzenegger, we can observe all five levers
working together. For instance, due to Schwarzenegger's
type, he often plays the role of the guy who overcomes all
odds. He epitomizes the American ideal. We find in him
a "typical" Saturn-Mars body type, with it's aggressive,
blunt, yet paternal tendencies: the silver – gold alchemy, an
aesthetic that is refined but rough enough to absorb abusive
falls; the chief features of dominance and power, with their
irresistible urge to take command of any situation, be it
friendly or hostile; the center of focus in the instinctive
part of the moving center, with it's equal ability to be
strong and agile especially under great pressure.

Saturn – Mars

Don't worry if this seems a bit complex at present...we'll
break these components down one by one and demonstrate

how they make sense as the parts begin to fit together. Foundation Knowledge is alive, an evolving Rubick's cube. You'll enjoy putting the pieces of the puzzle together as you study yourself, those around you, animals, plants, insects, etc., etc., etc.

As delineated earlier Foundation Knowledge pre – dates that time when European and Asian countries first began planning marriages and compatibility was crucial to insuring the viability of family lineage. Today, failed marriages and volatile or rather inharmonious work environments are due largely to a lack of understanding with regards to the human types and their tendencies. Individuals are continually entering into situations of undesirable cohabitation at home, work and play. Wonderful screenplays and scripts are being sabotaged by inappropriate casting and society as a whole is depriving itself of a better quality of life and evolution. In today's world, where environments are becoming somewhat homogenized, it's wise to use this method of understanding to avoid costly mistakes. Film making and business startups are so expensive that one can hardly afford the luxury of miscasting or office conflicts. Foundation Knowledge can be likened to a psychological immune system. By employing the Knowledge we can avoid a great deal of unnecessary pain, suffering and waste, which is usually manifested in the form of stress, selfishness and excessive therapy bills.

Though most, if not all, of the Knowledge contained in On The Elephant's Knee can be verified to be true, On The Elephant's Knee is not "the" truth; rather, it's a pair of eyes enabling us to better recognize those who would keep the truth from us.

Body Type

Origins Of Body Type

According to Foundation Knowledge, at the point of conception, the strongest influence on an individual's future behavior arises from one of the first five planets, the Sun, or the Moon. This yields seven types in all: the aggressive Martial, the cunning Mercury, the jolly Jovial, the dominating Saturn, the withdrawn Lunar, the nonexistent Venusian, the sparkling Solar.

That the alignment and constitution of the planets at conception determine body type is difficult to verify. We do know, however, that the gravitational pull of the moon has a tremendous effect on the tides and exerts a decided influence on the fluids in our bodies. We know that a full moon or new moon intensifies anxiety, evokes more extremes in the way we react; that the barometric pressure in the air affects our moods; that everything in the universe emanates energy; that traffic, subways or planes overhead affect us; that when somebody passes us on the street, we have a reaction, yet rarely notice it. Although we cannot see specifically how each person we contact, or each part of our environment, or each "vibration" or emanation from someone or something we encounter specifically contributes to what we say, feel and do, we must concede that they do affect us.

Suffice it to say that five of the planets, the Moon and the Sun provide convenient archetypes for the major kinds of personalities found among people. Not only the color and geography, but also the mythological associations of each of these heavenly bodies bears striking correspondence to specific types of human bodies.

For example, the planet Mercury is spinning quickly and the Mercury's mind is always active, often scheming, never at rest. Mars is a ruddy planet, which looks destructive, and Martial people are often rough and ruddy, with destructive, aggressive or martial tendencies. The two largest planets in the Solar System are Jupiter and Saturn; Jovials and Saturns are the body types with the largest body frames. As Jupiter and Saturn host many dependents, moons, rings and asteroids, so Jovials and Saturns tend to be paternal types, with large families and many friends. The Moon, round and pale, suggests the round, pale face which is typical of Lunar. Venus is a secretive planet, clouded over, its surface hidden by swirling gases; Venusians have a kind of shroud over their personalities that doesn't allow them to be seen, even to themselves. In a group they're almost invisible, as though they don't exist. The Sun is not a planet but a star, and Solar types are like sunlight: they are energetic, bright and lack a sense of solidity. They seem like butterflies floating on air rather than like stones, bears or trees.

We do not choose our type; we are born a Martial, Mercury, or a Jovial. This does not, however, imply a frigid and immutable system of predestination. In fact, Foundation Knowledge is alive. It grows, becomes more expansive and diverse in us as we absorb and apply it. To verify this we first note Body Type is a tendency, a behavioral trait that tends to predominate. It is by observing and verifying the tendency in action that we become masters of that tendency, just as in psychoanalysis and therapy, one gains control of neurotic symptoms by becoming aware of them. Second we have all the types within us. This qualification makes Foundation Knowledge a more flexible, useful tool than conventional astrology, in that the individual has the opportunity to move from a Mercury personality to a Solar and back again; she is not frozen into the mold of an "Aquarius," "Scorpio" or other astrological type. Given this mobility, it is also true that in most situations, one body type predominates; one body type overshadows all others, from the moment of birth until the moment of death. The human race collectively embodies all of the types, and any individual will manifest each of the types periodically throughout his or her life.

Identifying Body Type

To determine body type one of the first questions one can ask is, "Am I active or am I passive?" Active types create or initiate action; passive types withhold or absorb action. The second question one can ask is, "Am I positive or am I negative?" The positive type tends to be cheerful, optimistic, forward-looking; sees what is in the picture, rather than what is missing; tends to feel satisfied with what is present, rather than lamenting what is absent. Positive types tend to be supportive. Instead of "yes, but" a positive will say, "yes, fine, "or, "that's all right with me."   Positive types will manifest agreement right away, or at least benign indifference.

The negative type tends to view the glass of water as half empty rather than half full; sees what is missing; knows what needs to be done; has a sense of boundaries, limitations. A negative type is someone who "mismatches" whatever is presented to him. For example, you say, "It's a nice day," and the negative type responds, "Yeah, but it's a little cloudy." Negative types will almost always have a "yeah, but." They have to say "no" to everything first, or, "I disagree." They are not violently opposed, but simply not in agreement. Even if they do agree, their first instinct will be to disagree.

The positive types can be viewed as either easy-going or annoying. Similarly, the negative types can be seen as either irritating (the voice of doom-and-gloom) or realistic.

Likewise, active types can be seen as energetic and sponta-neous, or as interfering and aggressive. Passive types can be viewed as either thoughtful or lumbering and slow. In short, active, passive, negative and positive are not "good" or "bad" tendencies in and of themselves; they are just tendencies. Our goal in this study of types is not criticism or judgment—rather, observation and the acquisition and application of self-knowledge.

Body Type & The Enneagram

In the chart below, A stands for Active, P for Passive, + for Positive, and - for Negative.

Planet	Type	Characteristics
1. Moon	Lunar	P-
2. Venus	Venusian	P+
3. Mercury	Mercury	A-
4. Saturn	Saturn	A+
5. Mars	Martial	A-
6. Jupiter	Jovial	P+
7. Sun	Solar (Central)	A+

(A-) Martial	(P+) Jovial
(A+) Saturnine	(P-) Lunar
(A-) Mercurial	(P+) Venusian

The body types circulate within a diagram known as the "Enneagram:" *See page 29.*

Enneagram

The enneagram is an archetypal hieroglyphic symbol of a universal symbolic language containing within its diagrammatic representation the summation of the totality of the primary laws of the universe. It was said by Gurdjieff that this symbol was revealed to him by monks in an ancient, hidden monastery, perhaps the Sarmoung Monastery mentioned previously. A correct understanding of the laws of interpretation of this diagram will allow one to recognize and understand the fundamental nature and process of any phenomenon in the universe, as well as its interrelations with all other phenomena.

The enneagram is composed of three archetypal symbols. First is the circle, the symbol of Unity or Oneness, the completion of one full cycle or the fulfillment of the process of manifestation of any phenomenon whether microcosmic or macrocosmic. In many traditions this Unity is called God or the Absolute, in the Vedic tradition it is the Samhita, in the Egyptian, Nun, the primal unmanifest cosmic ocean.

Second is the equilateral triangle, the representation of what Gurdjieff referred to as the law of Three, called in India the Mother because of its role as the creator of manifest reality out of the transcendent powers of Unity, the circle. The Law of Three is the universal law of manifestation of force through polarity, with its triune aspects of positivity, negativity, and neutrality. This law is seen represented symbolically in every traditional system, such as in the Christian Holy Trinity, the Hindu triumvirate of Brahma, Vishnu and Shiva (the creative, preserving and destructive forces of nature), the Vedic Tishi, Devata and Chandaas, and the Egyptian Atum-Re, Shu and Tefnut. It is also seen in modern science in the protons, neutrons and electrons of chemistry , in the threefold constituents of atomic physics called quarks, and in the three primary colors of the light spectrum.

The third archetypal pattern represents what Gurdjieff called the Law of Seven, or the Law of Octaves. All of reality is composed of vibratory frequencies, and the law of Seven, also called the law of Vibration is the fundamental archetypal matrix upon which every manifest form in the cosmos from the most subtle to the most dense is constructed. The Law of Octaves also defines every process and relationship in the universe, being the foundation of all natural law and universal order. Manifestations of this law of nature can be seen in the seven notes of the musical scale, the seven colors of the rainbow, the seven chakras of the human psycho-physiological system, the seven Archangels and seven Elohim, universal creative powers, and of course, the seven sacred planets used in this system.

The combination of these three hieroglyphs creates the enneagram, a circle with nine points on the circumference, formed by the combination of the equilateral triangle and the symmetrical pattern of six flowing lines. These nine points are representative of the nine great principles of creation, called the Neteru in Egyptian cosmology or represented by the Tetraktys in Pythagorean cosmology (with the addition of the tenth point symbolizing Unity or completion as represented here by the circle). This fundamental cosmic calculator represents the relationship of Unity to the Law of Three and the Law of Seven, and a complete understanding of it allows the cognition of the essential nature of any phenomenon or process in the universe. The enneagram, in itself, is a complete cosmos, and every organism, form, or process, being a reflection or hologram of the wholeness of the cosmos may thereby be represented in its totality by the enneagram.

In the diagram to the right moving clockwise, we go from Lunar (P-) to Venusian (P+), to Mercury (A-), to Saturn (A+), to Martial (A-), to Jovial (P+), then back again to Lunar (P-). The Solar is fitted into the enneagram at the upper center.

Enneagram

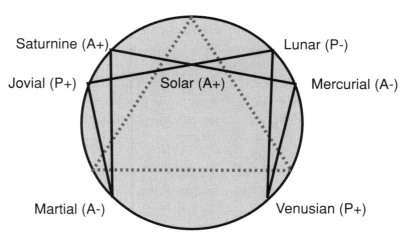

The type ahead of our type shows us where we are going, provides us with characteristics of another type which we can develop if we wish. This is called the "circulation" of types. For example, the Martial, which follows the Saturn on the enneagram, is the type most available to the Saturn. Thus, for the lumberous, indecisive, giant Saturn, the decisive, speedy Martial is a welcome change.

We can pick up qualities of all types, but the farther away the type is from ours on the enneagram, the more difficult it is for us to emulate. For example, it is difficult for a Jovial to pick up the perceptive cunning of the Mercury, while the quiet, poker-faced Lunar would find the Mercury's qualities more natural. The Jovial could go to the type behind it, the Martial, and pick up some tough, aggressive energy, but this is more difficult and less natural than going forward with the clockwise flow.

As we age, we naturally tend to pick up qualities of the type ahead of us. The cold Lunar tends to warm up and become more Venusian; the vegetative Venusian tends to seek out more spirited Mercury interests; the hectic Mercury begins to slow down and ponder as he enters Saturn; the Saturn finds decision-making less of a burden as he enters Mars; the aggressive impatience of the Martial will begin to relax as the Jovial influence expands; the gregarious Jovial finds the more conservative Lunar a nice change. The Solar can grow into any of the types.

The active and positive energies also circulate through the enneagram. The "active" energy follows the arrow from Mercury (A-) to Saturn (A+) to Martial (A-) to the "passive" energy flows from Jovial(P+) to Lunar(P-) to Venusian (P+). Solar is active (A+). In sum, we have two active negative types (the Mercury and the Martial, both A-), two passive positive types (the Jovial and the Venusian, both P+) and two active positive types (the Saturn and the Solar, both A+). The Lunar is the only passive negative type (P-).

Passive energy is "female" or receptive energy; active energy is "masculine" or aggressive energy. Again, this energy circulates around the enneagram. With the Lunar, the energy is most passive; with the Saturn, it is the most active. Lunars have the most feminine energy; whether they are males or females. Proceeding around the enneagram in the direction of the arrows, Venusians still have a lot of feminine energy but slightly more masculine energy; Mercuries have even more masculine energy. Saturns will be the most masculine of the types, whether they are males or females. Martials have only slightly more feminine energy than Saturns; then come the Jovials, and then we are back to the Lunars.

The Seven Body Types

LUNAR (P-) (Moon)

TYPICAL BODY: Lunars are pale, with roundish faces and a skin color that resembles the full moon. They tend to have peculiar bodies or unusual body proportions, such as: small chins, sloped or narrow shoulders, a long trunk with short legs.

EMOTIONAL MAKEUP: Lunars do not seem happy, though they are not unhappy. They may simply be absorbed in thought. Lunars do not express emotion outwardly, although they feel things intensely; instead they store up their emotions. They store and store their feelings and then release with a sudden outburst. If you are married to a Lunar, or have one as a sibling, child or parent, you will wonder why they have suddenly "blown up." You never knew they were angry, or hurt, or depressed. The expression of emotion seems to come "out of nowhere." That's the Lunar at work—absorbing everything, biding his or her time, quietly, secretly.

Lunars retreat when they are challenged. They like to go back to the old way—at least with the old way, they figure they are secure. They dislike change and, being essentially timid, can be caring and devoted particularly to existing traditions.

Lunars enjoy morbidity: like finding the worm in the apple. They enjoy, for example, fascinating tales about psychopaths, as well as horror films. It is not the violence that attracts them, but the interesting deviations. Lunars take pleasure in the grotesque. They often like little cubby holes, corners, houses with small rooms, being in the shade rather than the sun. They enjoy working at night and are quite devoted. They tend to work long hours. Lunars are reliable; they show up on time and rarely complain. You can count on a Lunar.

EXAMPLES; Famous Lunars include; Buster Keaton, Woody Allen, Mahatma Gandhi, George Bush, Queen

31

Elizabeth II. (Lunar-Venusians include: Rajiv Gandhi, John Major, Prince Charles). The American actor James Spader exemplifies the Lunar: a negative type, often passive, generally erratic, slightly loony. Indeed, Spader has mentioned in interviews that he enjoys playing the negative characters. He is often the evil conscience of the film. Because he is a negative type, he would naturally be more comfortable playing roles where a negative character is portrayed. Of course, this does not mean that a negative type is limited by his type to playing negative characters; it simply means the actor will be drawn to, and will seem most natural in those roles.

President Bush is a Lunar and so is Justice Souter. Souter, a quiet, withdrawn, private man naturally appealed to Mr. Bush's own psyche and seemed a natural choice for the Supreme Court.

Bush's Lunar tendencies became apparent in policy-making decisions. For example, when Gorbachev was being dethroned by the hard-line insurrectionists, Bush was asked how he would respond to the crisis. He said he would be "calm and firm." Lunars are often calm and firm, even during an emergency. Bush's foreign policy is characterized by a reliable coolness manifesting the Lunar's willfulness; it is also timid and withdrawn, manifesting the passive side. Bush tends to pull in, rather than radiate out. Under pressure Lunars can, and often do, just shut down. This passivity on Bush's part helped Gorbechev to liberalize the Soviet Union as it reduced his fear of being attacked by the West. Without provocation passive types do not have the energy to attack. Lunars often act by consensus, consulting confidantes and friends before finalizing a decision. Lunar tendencies also exist in nations, sports, modes of entertainment and politics. For example, the Chinese are a Lunar race. They conquer by absorption and secrecy.

Chess is a Lunar sport; you won't find many Lunars on the

Lunar

Lunar-Venusian

football field. Card-playing is Lunar (the poker-face is a Lunar invention: secretive, reclusive, hidden). Lunars are a watery type; they enjoy swimming and are good at water sports; but they don't like to compete. They like being near water.

IN SOCIETY: As Lunars represent the fullest embodiment of the feminine principle, Lunar women are extremely feminine, passive and soft. The moon and its phases affects Lunar moods more strongly than it does other types. Lunar women are very devoted. It's hard for them let go of a relationship. Lunars prefer the security of what is known about an existing spouse over risking the unknowns of a new spouse. (Mercuries, Martials and Solars; the active types tend to have many relationships.) Lunar women allow the man to be as strong as he wants. They are not interested in the soft, sensitive male, but prefer the wholesome masculine type. Lunar men tend to be effeminate and are often mistaken for homosexuals. Similarly, Saturn women often possess macho characteristics and are mistaken for lesbians. These types may think of themselves or be perceived as homosexual or lesbian when they are not.

"I don't like surprises" is a typical Lunar line in a relationship. Lunars crave consistency, safety and a sense of security. They are smooth and regular; they dislike shocks. Habit and repetition characterize the Lunar and they would rather remain in stasis than change. Lunars are mysterious with their inner most feelings hidden from us like the dark side of the moon. Only Lunars can know Lunars.

VENUSIAN (P+) (Venus)

TYPICAL BODY: Venusians are distinguished by thick hair and hairy bodies. They generally have dark hair, are often plump or overweight, may appear pear-shaped. The Venusian type is earthy and warm, gritty and vital. (In general, people with a lot of body hair are either Venusian, instinctively-centered or have a copper-silver alchemy; because hair is related to earthiness, solidness, and organicness). Also, like the Earth Mother, or fertility goddesses, Female Venusians often have large breasts and Rubenesque bodies.

EMOTIONAL MAKEUP: Venusians tend to be sympathetic and caring. They will put their arms around people, need to touch, to communicate, to protect, to express affection and understanding.

Many Venusians are in the healing professions: doctors, masseuses, chiropractors. "Good old-fashioned Southern hospitality"—the Southern ability to treat every stranger as an honored guest— is a Venusian tendency. The Venusian warmth and relaxed pace of the Southerner may feel smothering to active types, such as the Mercurial New Yorker, but this reflects the active type's perspective. To the Venusian Southerner, the active types are rude, abrupt and pushy, talk "too fast" and are always in a hurry.

You will find Venusians sitting on a porch, drinking and smoking, swinging and simply watching the day go by. Venusians are sedentary and tend to seek relaxation. Unlike the active types, they dislike exertion. Taking a warm bath at the end of the day is a typically Venusian activity.

The propensity of Venusians to relax can make them lazy, slothful. They often spill food or drink on their clothes, tables, chairs or other people. They tend to be careless dressers. Moreover, the Venusian's passivity can lead to indecisiveness, or at least, caution before a decision. They are the "may be," the "eventually," the "perhaps" type. The "Manana" syndrome (I'll do it tomorrow) is a Venusian concept of time. Where Martials act, Venusians procrastinate. The adaptive, absorptive and non-exerting qualities of the Venusians help them change characters as if they were actors. Venusians and Solars find it easier to adapt to new roles and new identities.

In fact, they actually graft the new identity onto themselves. They are the most flexible types, most capable of being or becoming whatever is needed.

EXAMPLES: Famous Venusians include Elizabeth Taylor, Sophia Loren, Zsa Zsa Gabor, the Goddess Venus. (Venusian-Mercury types include, Donald Trump, Robert DeNiro, Al Pacino, Dustin Hoffman, Burt Reynolds, Barbara Hershey, Barbara Streisand, Bill Clinton, Frank Sinatra, Francois Mitterrand, Saddam Hussein, Muammar Kaddefi.)

Eastern philosophies often express Venusian tendencies and indeed, there are many Venusians in the East. The Buddha, for instance, is depicted in sitting position. He may be mentally active, but physically, the posture expresses inertness, stillness. This tendency may be seen in contrast to that of the United States, a Saturn-Mars nation. It is difficult for Americans to sit still.

In general, the United States consists of active, aggressive types. Bringing in an eastern philosophy where you're supposed to sit, meditate, relax and let everything flow through you and out of you; a Gandhian view of society cannot work in America. Americans need to meditate while they are running because they're not going to be able to sit down. Martial arts are much more acceptable to Westerners; they will prefer Chuck Norris and karate movies to documentaries on the life of the Buddha; football games to nature walks and incense.

Venusians and Venusian-Mercury politicians generally do not fare well in America, since warmth and sympathy, pleasant as they are, do not equate into acts of "doing." The Saturn-Mars Americans may desire sympathy but they need obvious, direct, and forceful action. Thus far, most of America's successful and more popular presidents have been centered around the Saturn and Mars types. Walter Mondale and Michael Dukakis are Venusian-Mercury. People distrusted these men the way they distrusted Nixon. The Venusian

Lunar-Venusian

Venusian-Mercury

Venusian-Mercury

Venusian-Mercury-Solar

side of the Venusian-Mercury personality will be soft and caring while the devious, Mercury side is often short sighted and selfish. One never knows what the Mercurial, shrouded behind the Venusian non-existence, is thinking.

The Mercury says one thing, but is thinking something else, or thinking twenty things. This may not be bad, but because of the speed of their thoughts you know something else is going on, and you don't trust them.

IN SOCIETY: Venusians are warm and caring in a relationship. They make people feel secure, and unconditionally accepted. They are consistently affectionate, and cannot be shaken emotionally. Once they commit, they stick around. They are steady, though unlike Lunars. A Lunar is steady like a Swiss clock; Venusians provide a stream of unending warmth. These same qualities can make them appear smothering. As we noted earlier, our impression of other types is conditioned by our own type. The qualities of a passive type can appear as negatives to a negative type; the qualities of an active type negative to a passive type.

Socially, Venusians tend to non-exist. They are the ones you forget to count or call, the ones whose names you can never remember, the ones you don't see even if they are standing in front of you. They dislike arguments and they love food and touching.

MERCURY (A-)

TYPICAL BODY: Mercuries are frequently small in build. They tend to have dark hair and bright or slightly bulging neon eyes. Mercuries are often clean and tidy. Male Mercuries often like to hide behind a trim mustache or beard. And Mercuries can have deep, honey-tone voices that soothe the listener. This is more true of Venusian-Mercury than the pure Mercury. Mercuries also tend to have pointed facial features: the nose, the eyebrows, the corners of the lips, the chin, and ears. Often the arms and legs will be angular or sharp and pointy.

EMOTIONAL MAKEUP: In Greek mythology, Mercury is the messenger, the winged god. Mercuries are active, meaning that they are external in their behavior; outgoing or extroverted. They are pushy, rather than withdrawn.

Mercuries like bright colors. They are sly, cunning, and quick. They have many thoughts at once, often speak rapidly, are perceptive, and have many ideas in quick succession. However, few of these ideas exist in depth. Mercuries tend toward surface knowledge. They can size up a person quickly; gather a lot of information on many subjects. Then have trouble retaining the information. Mercuries also tend to be more paranoid than other types because they think others are as devious as they are. The Mercurial is the most outwardly critical of the seven types making sure that others know when it's unhappy, irritated, or disappointed. They are the 'baby type" prone to complaining and whining, as would a child if they can't have things their way.

The machine gun is a Mercurial invention, and an appropriate metaphor for this body type as Mercuries are a speedy, rapid thinking, quick reaction type.

EXAMPLES: Famous Mercuries include Sammy Davis Jr., James Woods, Michael Milken and rock star, Prince. (Mercury-Saturn types include *Star Trek's* Mr. Spock, Ivan Lendl, Jawaharial Nehru, Ivan Boesky.) Richard Nixon ("Tricky Dick"), the sly politician, is the archetypal Mercury. The Mercurial, because it assumes it can outsmart the other types, underestimates the prowess of the other types. "You're too smart for your own good" is often said to Mercury, because they often end up outsmarting themselves and getting caught by their own deviousness.

IN SOCIETY: In addition to their short-sightedness,

Mercury-Saturn

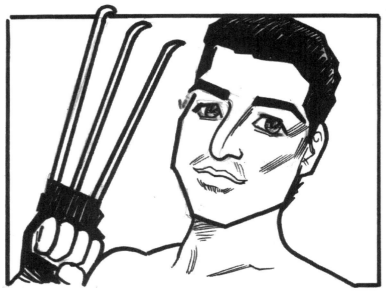

Mercury-Saturn

Mercuries have a problem with vanity: they like people to know how sly they are, tendency which can and does bring them unwanted exposure, as in the case of Richard Nixon. Mercuries, as the baby of the types, like babies, need more attention to feel secure. The planet Mercury is closest to the sun, and in a sense receives more attention from the sun than do the other planets.

Many Mercuries do things to let people know they are deceitful. And they assume those who they deceive can and will do nothing to them, will not catch them. This escape from punishment feeds their vanity and encourages them to remain as they are.

Mercuries tend to interrogate, rather than simply ask questions. They like to spy on people. The Mercury thinks manipulatively, deviously. Mercuries are always acting, and do, in fact, make good actors.

Mercuries enjoy entertaining others as a ploy to attract attention. Yet they are dangerous in positions of influence, because they are often in that position to gain attention rather than to exercise prudent authority.

Internally a Mercurial would tend to see a political career as a form of self-entertainment. Mercurials need support and approval more often then they can give it. As politicians they are interested in what the voters can do for them, more than what they can do for the voters.

Mercuries have little long-term vision, and are often chasing short-sighted gains. They are charming and perceptive but often selfish and self-motivated, like children.

Mercuries are sexually charged. They expend this sex energy through heated conversation, quick repartees and rapid shifts of attention. They are always debating, will never agree with you. They do not like to be caught; they would rather zigzag than be trapped into one position. They appear always to be hiding something, as if there is subtext behind their statements. They are good communicators, yet often magnify faults in others in an effort to conceal their own. More than other types, the Mercurial and Martial types reject the concept of body types.

In addition to their highly perceptive tendencies, ability to obtain vast amount of information, we also find in the Mercurial type a tireless promoter, hard-working, bright, and a spontaneous element which cheers and refreshes.

SATURN (A+)

TYPICAL BODY: The Saturn is a tall, lethargic, big boned person who tends to dominate in his environment. His mental outlook (due in part to the fact that he is tall), is one of overview, long-distance planning, and formality. Even when a Saturn is short in stature, he projects enormity and dominance and is perceived as being taller than he actually is. A Saturn woman might be 5'6" or 5'7" or maybe 5'8", but she will seem taller than those around her. Saturn's often have large feet, longer noses, longer faces, high cheek bones and long fingers.

EMOTIONAL MAKEUP: Saturns tend to ponder everything; rarely making a quick, spontaneous decision. For example, if you suggest going out to dinner, and your spouse is a Saturn, he or she will agonize over which restaurant to visit, which dish to order, what to drink, what to have for dessert, and then, which is the best road home. Through this excessive hesitation, Saturns make others wait, which finds them more time to convince others to agree with them, to think like them, to be dominated by them. Saturns are subject to self-denial yet behind the self-denial is a belief that they must first dominate themselves before they have a right to dominate others.

Though Saturns are an active type they tend to be hesitant,

slow, lumbering, in need of a push before making a decision. Saturns loathe making mistakes. They would rather change the rules, since admitting failure implies a lack of vision and an additional expenditure of energy. Saturns dislike wasting their energy. They assume others make mistakes while they follow the program. Frugality and order are important to them. Saturns have an intense urge to follow rules and make others follow as well. They will try to convince you that what is good for them is good for you. They express a controlled logic that is often practical but difficult to absorb emotionally. They crave propriety: everything in its place, in the right time, and under their dominance.

Because of their over-view, Saturns are often in positions of authority. The good news is that their ponderousness has a valuable side. It allows them to consider many options fully and equally. Thus, they are often leaders in business or government.

Female Saturns are often found in the modeling profession.

EXAMPLES: famous Saturns include Abraham Lincoln, Michael Jordan, Larry Byrd, Billy Graham, Charles de Gaulle, Cheryl Tieggs, Julie Andrews. (Saturn-Mars types include Ronald Reagan, Helmut Kohl, Clint Eastwood, Charleton Heston, Chris Everett, Stephi Graff.) Princess Diana epitomized the Saturn woman: tall big-boned, dominant yet cautious. The Saturn fills a room he or she enters and is typically noticed by most people.

Basketball players are often Saturn; so are giants. Michael Jordan recently described himself as a 'gentle giant." The "Jolly Green Giant" of frozen vegetable fame is a classic Saturn. They are big people but not overpowering like the active negative types. They may dominate, yet rarely beat people up. You'll find many of these types in fairy tales.

IN SOCIETY: The Saturn and Saturn-Mars types reflect the current American vision of female beauty. Centuries ago,

Saturn-Mars

Saturn-Mars

Saturn-Mars

Saturn-Mars

the Venusian female was the ideal: lush, round, lusty, "Reubenesque." Today, magazines and movies tout the "hard-body" female, taut and toned. The Saturn-Mars is the ideal of masculinity as well. A man must be tough, strong, defend the home, and so on. (A Lunar man, such as George Bush, will feel less accepted in a Saturn-Mars society.) The society will reject the softness, the introversion, the passivity. Although the Saturn type reflects the ideal, masculine women (Saturns) and feminine men (Lunars) may feel out of place expressing their tendencies in such a society, even though it's normal for a Saturn woman to like cowboy boots, to prefer jeans to dress-es and to enjoy playing with toy soldiers rather than dolls.

Exercise programs help individuals create the ideal Saturn-Mars body. Thus, women throughout our world (due to America's influence) are being taught that they need to be more like men to compete with men; that being "feminine"— or perhaps, Venusian—won't work in a market that is a com-petitive-orientated environment. The Katherine Hepburn personality is "in": craggy, masculine features, a harsh voice, snappy come-backs. But Asian women tend to be Lunar-Venusian and Venusians in general have softer, more rounded bodies. Their societies traditionally cultivate the feminine— not only in women but also in men.

A pure Saturn woman is the midpoint of masculinity. Many Saturns can appear androgynous. The females like to wear men's clothes and enjoy somber attire; gray, plain, drab cloth-ing relaxes and protects them.

A Saturn-Mars female, with the martial element influence in her, will be slightly more aggressive than a pure Saturn female. The Saturn-Mars female will be more determined in her walk, how she speaks, raises her children, buys clothes, thinks, etc.

MARTIAL (A-) (Mars)

TYPICAL BODY: Martials frequently have a reddish or ruddish skin tone, freckles, crooked teeth, and skin or back problems. They can be bowlegged and often have red or light colored hair.

EMOTIONAL MAKEUP: You can always spot the Martial: he or she is the one taking the offensive. Martials are aggressive: they prefer the straightest path to any goal. They are warriors in most situations, elevating to the level of war even with the smallest struggle or challenge. Martials like a challenge, glorify struggle, and crave independence, their own space and territory. An instinctively centered Martial with a chief feature of power is the most territorial of all the types. And Martials not only defend their territory they actively seek to expand it, even to the point of self-destruction. Martials cannot contain themselves, nor can they be contained. Martials and Mercuries, the two active negative types, are responsible for most wars. The ancient Vikings, Romans, German, Turks, and the Irish, are all Martial races. Martials are explosive and un-diplomatic. Everything for them is urgent, must be done now, and at once.

Martials hate being dominated and they resist any perceived chains. While defined environments make Saturns and the three passive types feel safe and comfortable, such definition imprisons the Martial by making him feel claustrophobic. Where the Saturn type is stoic, the Martial is spontaneous, discordant and aggressive.

Martials take pleasure in destructiveness and turmoil. Indeed, destructiveness is the chief feature of this particular body type (although individuals within the type have varying chief features). Martials tend to be blunt and direct and these qualities help them succeed in business. Martials like giving and receiving orders, not because they like being told what to

48

Mars-Solar

Mars-Solar

do, but because orders are direct, straight and clear. What could be more direct than an order. If you want to hire somebody to achieve goals, hire a Martial.

Martials often make good sales people because they are aggressive, relentless and dismissive of obstacles. They also excel in sports. They are goal-oriented and will continue working until they run out of energy, rather than stop when a job is done. This is one reason why Martials tend to be destructive. They go past a goal. Like closing a door so hard you pull off the handle.

EXAMPLES: Famous Martials include Margaret Thatcher (the "Iron Lady"), Hillary Clinton, Glenda Jackson, Jane Fonda, Madonna, Ross Perot, Oliver North, Chuck Norris, John McEnroe, Borris Becker, J.F.K., Maneka Gandhi, Bruce Springsteen, Mike Tyson. (Mars-Jovial types include Winston Churchill, Benny Hill, Red Skelton, Albert Einstein, Walt Whitman, Hemingway, Boris Yeltsin.)

Martials are tough and concentrated people you don't want to disagree with because to disagree would invite a confrontation.

Martial women often have a concomitant difficulty expressing their femininity. They stand in sharp relief to the warm, sympathetic Venusian beauties, such as Elizabeth Taylor, Sophia Loren and Marilyn Monroe, for whom little or no effort is required.

Yet Martial women do have their own formula for sexiness, exemplified by Madonna, whose sex-appeal springs from her aggressiveness. Martial women demand sex; they do not ask or wait for it. Martial women enjoy Venusian men who let them run the show; yet at the same time, they tire of always overpowering men. Madonna's attraction to effeminate men is the Martial in her being attracted to a passive element. Martial women often feel a need to prove their femininity by demonstrating sex appeal, by acting sexy rather than by being sexy.

The Martial's destructiveness also has positive qualities. Changing or challenging fixed ideas, stagnate beliefs, hopes and dreams helps people to grow, to learn where change seemed impossible. This is destructiveness in the best sense: it is not negative; it means stirring the water where it has become stagnate.

IN SOCIETY: Also on the positive side, the Martial's matter-of-fact bluntness can make them extremely effective in work situations. A Martial will provide a no-nonsense, trailblazing approach that is easy to follow. Martials thrive on overcoming obstacles. Moreover, they are often good for their word. They are honest and reliable, and insist on punctuality. Martials are often the marshals in society.

The United States (a Saturn-Mars country similar to the ancient Romans and following in their footsteps toward becoming Venusian-Mercury), dominates the world economically and culturally, and generally wins wars when a Martial or a Saturn-Mars is leading the nation. General Schwartzkof (Stormin' Norman), is a Saturn-Mars; his Saturn overview of the strategic situation in Iraq, combined with his Martial aggressiveness, were powerful factors in his military successes. Patton, Washington, Eisenhower were also Saturn-Mars, and thus in harmony with the nation's type. Martials love guns, the acquisition of power through force or destructiveness. Alexander the Great was a Saturn-Mars type.

And those in harmony with a nation's type will find it less difficult to succeed in that Nation, some of America's most successful actors are Saturn-Mars or Mars. Sylvester Stallone, in his role as Rambo, is almost Mars incarnate: thick biceps, the sweat of determination, the thrust for justice, the call of heavy artillery. Although Rambo projects a Martial image, Stallone himself is a Venusian-Mercury. His Martial roles are tempered by his Mercury cunning and Venusian sympathies.

Mars

Mars-Jovial

Schwarzenegger, a Saturn-Mars type, in contrast, is direct and honest. When he says "I'll be back," you do not doubt him. If Stallone said he was coming back, you'd wonder. Since the United States is a Saturn-Mars country, it sees itself more in Schwarzenegger than in Stallone. Small wonder Arnold Schwarzenegger is practically a cult figure in the U.S.

Americans like the way Schwarzenegger solves problems: straightforward, no tricks, do the job and go home. Stallone exhibits more cunning: his nickname is "Sly." This impresses Americans but does not evoke the cult ideology of Schwarzenegger. Saturn-Mars types do well in Saturn-Mars societies. They are less successful in Lunar, Venusian or Mercurial nations. The Japanese for example, fail to understand how Americans can love guns.

JOVIAL (P+) (Jupiter)

TYPICAL BODY: A Jovial is often a rounded or rubenesque figure, with a cheery face, a big head and pudgy nose. Fat comes naturally to Jovials. The extra weight, however, is not necessarily repulsive on Jovial; rather it fits them. Jovials tend to have bad eyesight, thicker fingers and hands. They are subject to periodicity, love music, the Arts and Literature.

Because they are flamboyant, gregarious and life-affirming, Jovials tend to have trouble losing weight. They also tend to lose their hair young. Jovial and Venusian women tend to have larger busts, particularly if they are emotionally-centered. If Saturns are tall, then Jovials are big, rounded people. And Jovials tend to be more rare as a type; which accounts in part, for them frequently having vanity as a chief feature.

EMOTIONAL MAKEUP: The Jovial is the happy type. They are flamboyant and generous, sometimes to a fault; they give away everything. They enjoy collecting knickknacks

Jovial-Lunar

Jovial-Lunar

and often live cluttered lives. They love to share, to make everyone happy. Jovial seeks to create emotional harmony wherever they go.

In contrast to Mercuries, who have a lot of superficial knowledge, the Jovial type seeks depth. For example, if you have a special chair in your home, a Jovial , if he has any interest in chairs, will know what kind of chair it is. He will inquire as to what century it was made, how its details compare with those of other chairs of its kind, what the varnish is, what kind of wood, and so on.

EXAMPLES: Famous Jovials included, Burl Ives, George Orwell, Falstaff, Benny Hill, W.C. Fields, Aretha Franklin and Shelley Winters (Jovial-Lunars included, India's P.M. Narashima Rao, Gorbachev, the Dalai Lama.)

We can see the influence of the Jovial type during holidays, especially Christmas for the West, Diwali in India and New Years throughout the world. Christmas began as a celebration of the birth of Christ, but now people feel forced to give gifts because it's become Jovial Day, rather than Christ's day. Santa Claus embodies the Jovial type. So does Friar Tuck. Both are big-bellied, generous souls whose hardy laugh shows a lust for life.

IN SOCIETY: Jovials act as a social lubricant. They make everyone happy. They display an ease and attraction, which disarms people and makes them comfortable. Jovials like people and are well liked and needed by people. They possess the "huggability" factor. Nothing is more comforting than a nice warm hug from a Jovial.

Although Jovials are harmonizing, they can also be overbearing. This is the down side of the Jovial type. (The same trait that makes each type so successful also has its negative aspect.) Jovials want to give gifts, to make sure everyone is happy. Such giving, if it becomes excessive can be intrusive. Moreover, Jovials can suffer from vanity. Because they are frequently deep, perceptive and informed they can be vain and superior about their knowledge. They are diverse but can become too proud of this diversity.

They don't see too much diversity as being a handicap. They think that they are more in tune with the world and that they are above problems that other people have. Jovials appear exempt from the sense of difficulty that other types seem never to be without. Jovials are an emotionally-orient-ed type. They like charities, family and social gatherings. The pleasure of learning and owning things excites them, and therefore Jovials tend to spend money freely. In addition, Jovials love to drink... but not by themselves.

SOLAR (A+)

TYPICAL BODY: Solars tend to have beautiful skin, almost translucent. They are often frail, thin-boned and prone to accidents and ill health. Frequently their eyes are further apart and a bit larger than in other types. Solar is the most refined of types, the least primitive and functional, where other types work, Solars play, rather than seeing something as serious Solars are amused. Unlike the other planetary types that tend to reserve energy like one would save money in a bank account, this unassociated planetary type spends all of its energy everyday.

EMOTIONAL MAKEUP: Solars are cheerful, efferves-cent, childlike. They are exciting to be around, ethereal, and often have naivete as a chief feature. When they do some-thing wrong, it's easy to forgive them. Because of their naivete we don't tend to see their mistakes as being terribly sinful. Moreover, because the negative or instinctive halves of the four centers are not well-developed in Solars, the other types do not react as negatively or defensively toward them.

Mars-Solar

Solar-Lunar

Undeveloped negative halves means that Solars lack decided instinctive reactions to conflict, danger, or emergencies. They see no reason to defend themselves. They tend to be impulsive, careless and incautious and are subject to dying young, to accidents, and to "burning out."

Solars are like a sunny day. When they enter our lives, we feel as though the sun has just come out. They have the qualities of innocence, defenselessness, cheerfulness, faith, and lightness. They are an active positive type. And Solar types are generally mixed with the six planetary types. A pure Solar is difficult to find, except in myth (Snow White, for example).

EXAMPLES: of Famous Solars include Michael Jackson, Nancy Reagan, Percy Bysshe Shelley, Mozart, Van Morrison, Judy Garland. (Solars mixed with other types include Whitney Houston as a Solar-Mercury, Buster Keaton a Lunar-solar, Marilyn Monroe a Venusian-Solar. Elvis Presley a Venusian-Mercury-Solar, Julia Roberts a Saturn-Mars-Solar, Bo Derek-Saturn-Mars-Solar, Michelle Pfeiffer a Mars-Solar. Paul Newman a Mars-Solar, Rajiv Gandhi a Lunar-Venusian-Solar, Sydney Poitier a Solar-Saturn-Mars, Robert Redford a Saturn-Mars-Solar, Lawrence Olivier a Solar-Saturn.

Goldie Hawn is classic "Solar": cheerful, innocent-looking, naive, wide-eyed. Solars look youthful, no matter what their age. Dick Clark is a good example.

Solars don't see problems; they are imaginative and playful; they seem to have no cares; theirs is a world of fantasy and dream, as this, to them, is more real than the "real world." They like cartoons, toys, and having fun. Hawn's roles are often fun incarnate.

IN SOCIETY: In the myth of Pandora's box every force in human affairs escaped from the box, but one thing remained: hope. Solars represent this hope. Everybody has some Solar in them, some bit of optimism that remains untouched by life's changing and often harsh circumstances. Even in a negative, dark city, full of crime, people will express their Solar part, exclaim not to worry, that all will be well; as Little Orphan Annie would say: "the sun will come out tomorrow." Because Solars are often non-threatening many people don't take them seriously. Yet Solars can be serious and their innocent and refreshing smiles, their optimistic positivity, can end winning them millions of adherents.

Maximum Attraction
Maximum Repulsion

In addition to revealing the circulation of types, the enneagram conveys another set of relationships: the types lying opposite each other tend to be most attracted to one another. This phenomenon is called, "maximum attraction." For example, the (P+) Venusian is the maximum attraction to the (A-) Martial. This means, in effect, that the direct, aggressive, decisive, forceful, Martial will, unconsciously, find in the soft, passive, earthy, relaxed Venusian all the things he or she would like to be but cannot be. Whether they are colleagues or lovers, Martials will be drawn to Venusians above all other types; Venusians will similarly be drawn to Martials, finding in them the qualities the Venusian he or she would like to possess.

Similarly the (A+) Saturn's maximum attraction, opposite on the Enneagram; is the (P-) Lunar. Saturn is dominant and obvious whereas the Lunar is passive and secretive. Saturns are effective administrators; Lunars have little overview. Saturns like regularity; monotony is a comfort to them. Lunars feel safe with Saturns; they know with a Saturn there won't be any sharp corners. They'll come home, watch the same television show, drink the same wine, make the same dinner.

The (P+) Jovial's maximum attraction is the (A-)

Maximum Attraction

Lunar-Venusian   *Saturn-Mars*

Mercury   *Jovial*

Maximum Repulsion

Mercury

Martial

Martial

Mercury

Mercury. The Jovial is large and fraternal, the Mercury small and cunning. The Jovial is giving, the Mercury is taking. The qualities that are lacking in one are fulfilled in another: opposites attract.

The Solar has no maximum attraction, which simply means that it can be attracted to any of the types and any type can be attracted to the Solar.

Maximum attraction also invites maximum repulsion. Although the Martial will be attracted to the Venusian because of the Venusian's warmth and sympathy, the Martial will have trouble with the Venusian's sloppiness, laziness and passivity. They will live out the dance of attraction and repulsion in everything they do. While maximum attraction has a romantic appeal, it is no panacea.

A different phenomenon occurs when two similar types are put together. Each will feel as though he or she knows everything about the other. A Martial who cuts people off on the freeway, prefers punk rock to classical music, enjoys Chuck Norris films, obvious leather attire and will be delighted to find in his or her partner the same preferences. Each will feel deeply understood and cared for. Yet, this same abundance of similarity can lead to stagnation, a feeling that there isn't much more to know about the other. After the initial spark of "finding a soulmate," the flame may die all too quickly.

At the summit of maximum repulsion are the two active negative types, the Martial and the Mercury. Both seek the same space and influence. They challenge each other for that space and influence. A challenge which too often becomes physically and emotionally violent.

Body Type & Sexuality

The knowledge of body type can increase our understanding of sexuality and love-making, and help to transform critical judgments or self-judgment into observation and acceptance. For example, Martials and Mercuries tend to have a greater sex drive than other types, because sex releases the active, negative energy which accumulates in their bodies.

Orgasm energy is similar to that of Martials and Mercuries. Apart from sex, the active, explosive and extroverted energy produced by all types is called Sex Energy. Sex Energy expresses itself in creative challenge, in extreme speech, provocative concepts, fervent crusades, fanatical enthusiasms. And Sex Energy becomes negative if it's confined for too long. Physical sex is comforting to the active negative types, and to instinctively centered people; it's like what they're like, so they feel good pursuing sex, having sex.

Active negative types like Martials will tend to change sexual partners frequently, whereas the passive types – Lunars, Jovials and Venusians – will prefer one wife, one "steady" boyfriend or girlfriend. The passive types enjoy stability in every aspect of their lives, sex life included; the active types will like variety, change different partners, sexual positions, settings. Venusians revel in the sensuality of sex, whereas Martials and Mercuries pursue sex to relieve negative pressure. The Solar's relationship to sex is more playful and innocent. They do not give it the same level of power that others may give it in terms of influence over other daily activities or values.

Further, we can see that each body type will prefer different activities with a spouse or lover on a typical night. A Martial for example will be out to hunt, confront and overpower his girl, or she her man, showing little interest in foreplay, or formalities. A Jovial will arrange or seek out a party, bring old friends together, play with the children. A Lunar will be closeted away with someone, cuddling in bed, or sitting around the fire reading books. A Mercury will be in some intellectual or political debate over dinner, or attend a movie to argue about its meaning. A Solar will be shopping for sweets (they love sugars), enjoying the stars, playing outdoors, or dancing in their living room to a favorite tune. A Venusian will just sit around, languishing over television, a warm summer night, or a good meal. A Saturn will be organizing something, pondering the course of world events, or doing taxes, writing papers putting everything under control.

Countries dominated by active types (Germany-France-Italy-Sweden-Australia) will tolerate greater promiscuity, as active types change sexual and romantic partners more frequently. The Lunar Chinese, Jovial-Lunar Russians, and Lunar-Venusian Indians have sexually conservative societies while a Saturn-Mars nation like the United States seeks to initiate "sexual revolutions."

Body Type & Career

Body types will be attracted to, and most comfortable in jobs and careers in harmony with their type. Knowledge of body type is useful to the career counselor or consultant, as well as helpful to the employer and employee.

Lunars like the privacy of late-night jobs, or jobs with little external confusion. They're very meticulous. They enjoy jobs that require detail, categorization: Ph.D. in Nuclear Physics, Anthropology; butterfly, stamp and coin collecting or cataloging every bone of a dinosaur. Lunars enjoy petite work, when everything is in focus and in close range. They're a tunnel vision type; reality is and must be close to them. They tend to enjoy jobs that are near-sighted: they become secretaries, proofreaders, editors. The publishing

Saturn

Mars

Jovial

Lunar

Venusian

Mercury

Solar

business has many Lunars. "Get one good job where you know the routine, have a reliable environment, can be meticulous" — that's a Lunar attitude.

Venusians enjoy jobs that don't make too many demands, because Venusians like to nonexist, and to relax. They want a steady job, a reliable job, one that doesn't require much energy. They become postal clerks, secretaries, bank tellers. Venusians like people — not in the same manner as Jovials (flamboyantly or gregariously), but in a warm and caring fashion. The medical profession attracts Venusians — nurses, doctor's aides, physical therapists. You won't find many Venusians in an emergency room, though you may find a Venusian-Mercury in such a situation, since it draws to the cunning and mental agility of the Mercury side. Venusian-Mercuries will be soothing and healing people — drawing on the Venusian side — but the patients will have gunshot wounds, some exciting medical problem that will draw on the Mercury's curious, quick mind. Within the healing professions, masseuses and chiropractors will tend to draw the more pure Venusians.

Mercuries are an active, energetic type so they will attract jobs that require active, energetic people. For example, Mercuries like acting, putting on a show. Many sales people are Mercuries, particularly car sales people. New York is a Mercury city, so it will provide many Mercury professions and draw many Mercuries to the area. Wall Street, for example, is Mercurial, with its quick action, rapid exchange of millions of dollars. Many talk show hosts are Mercury or Venusian-Mercury.

Mercuries use their perception frequently but not necessarily, to cheat or deceive people. Yet the Mercury's ability to portray matters divisively is not always a bad thing. If you're convicted of a crime, you'll want a Mercury to represent you in court. He'll be quick on his feet, respond ably to a judge, address a jury intelligently, and use his slyness overall to your benefit. We're not saying that a courtroom lawyer has the same qualities as a thief; simply that the tendencies of the body type are the same. Moreover, we're not talking about individuals but about types.

Saturns like jobs with authority. Any chance they can, they want to have either total authority or no authority. Any presidential job — head of the company, director of operations, person in charge of group — attracts Saturns. The British Empire exemplifies Saturn aspirations. The Brits came from a tiny country, yet were able to extend a web of dominance all over the world. They are plain, bland, people with little spontaneity, little color — yet excel at administrative control. Saturn's are the 'gray' type.

The Saturn is a somber, self controlled stoic type which prefers understatement, caution and regularity. The English have a play, "No Sex Please — We're British." They keep a "stiff upper lip." Saturns will look for jobs that allow them to be stoic, somber, ponderous, cautious. They will be managers, teachers, chairman, coaches, captains, presidents, the head of landscaping crew, head of the fire department, head of the clean-up detail... Saturns don't feel good unless they have a dominant position, and they feel more justified than others in taking a dominant position.

Martials will attract the work of football players, cops, businessmen, boxers; any kind of active, aggressive job will appeal to Martials. Martials make good soldiers, fire fighters, truck drivers, woodsmen, ranchers, lawyers. A Martial lawyer will be different from a Mercury lawyer. The Mercury will be putting together the brilliant brief, outmaneuvering his opponent. The Martial will be much more blunt, assertive, straight-forward. He'll enjoy the battle as much as the result. An intellectually-centered Martial can exert so much intellectual aggression it may feel physical and cause others to react physically. He'll be the one trying to humiliate his opponent

in front of the jury.

Indeed, Martials are attracted to law because they are direct and open with a strong need to experience the adrenaline of justice. Martin Luther King, John F. Kennedy, and Jesse Jackson are in this league: interested in social justice, in the right of the victim to attain justice. Martials demand fairness, as the Old Testament prophets did. (Mercuries will express their sense of "justice" by not paying taxes, or going around the rules, as in Watergate.)

Jobs that permit the employee to be honest, blunt and direct will attract Martials. As a type, they are attracted to visible justice. Visibility in this sense is blunt. Martials like being physical, territorial, even if they are emotionally or intellectually focused. Overcoming obstacles invigorates them. "We shall overcome" is a Martial concept. People who work in logging tend to be Martials: they like to be challenged by a physical obstacle. They like trail-blazing.

Martial women will be more macho or boyish, with a more unrefined masculinity than Saturn women. Women cowboys, women entrepreneurs, taxi drivers, weight lifters, sanitation workers, construction workers, etc., epitomize the Martial woman. A chief executive woman, if she is Martial: will want to be in power and change things. She'll often demonstrate the fact that she's the boss. With a Saturn, you'll know, intuitively that he or she is the boss. The Martial will tell you directly, that if you don't do what you're told to do , you'll get fired.

Jovials since they are an emotionally-centered type, will enjoy people-oriented jobs: social workers, marriage counselors, and musicians are often Jovial or around Jovial. Anything that puts them in contact with people, especially if they can be helpful. Charities are big for Jovials. Being involved in a church or synagogue. Putting together a social event. Being in a position where they can be benevolent to people.   Again, social work.   Working on the Olympics. United Nations work.   The U.N. is itself a Jovial concept, Jovials will like Earth day.   Saving the planet.   Harmonizing all nations.

Solars in having a lot of naivete, innocence and carefree-ness, would welcome any job that permits them to be irre-sponsible, to enjoy themselves.   Kindergarten teacher, day-care instructor, toy-maker, cartoonist, these are good Solar professions.   Hostesses at restaurants manifest the Solar, as do cheerleaders and ushers at weddings, though Solars would always like to be the bride or groom.   Resorts and hotels often employ Solars; or maybe you'll find Solar in your favorite wait-ress at the local diner, the one who has known you for years and is always cheerful to her customers.

But in all this its difficult to generalize as each body type can have a different alchemy, center of focus and chief feature.   For example, we'll have an intellectually-centered Martial becom-ing a lawyer; and emotionally-centered Martial throwing tem-per tantrums on the job or with his spouse in public; a mov-ing-centered Martial becoming a cop; an instinctively-cen-tered Martial becoming a wrestler or weight lifter.   When we talk about jobs, there are so many factors that come into play that we must generalize. But the distinctions are still useful. A Martial social worker, for example, will be aggressive: intrud-ing on families, trying to prevent domestic violence.   A Venusian will be warm and caring, dropping by just to say hello. Moreover, the Solar type, because it mixes so well with all the types, enjoys the ability to take on a variety of jobs and roles.

In addition, environmental factors effect the choices a type might make. For example, if you're Lunar and you live in a small town in Ohio and there's only one postal clerk in town and that was the job for you, you might have to find something less suited to your type. If you're the postal clerk and you're a

Martial, but you got the job because your father and grandfather before you had it; you may be uncomfortable with your choice. You'll find many people in jobs that are not in harmony with their type out of circumstance, or economic realities. Let's say you want to play tennis but in your town, there are no tennis courts. Tennis is a perfect game for your type, but all you can do is run races.

Or you're in a law firm: you might enjoy doing research in a corner of the library (Lunar), but you're needed in court to argue like a Mercury or Martial. Or you're a child and you dream of playing the piano, but your father forces you to take up violin. You may become an accomplished musician, but there will be more intimacy, more of your essence, more life in your music when you turn to the piano. That's where the "magic" comes from in a performance, musical or otherwise. Many people get into jobs without realizing the influence of type and their happiest days are vacations.

Blended Body Types

When we described each body type in some detail, we focused on pure types. These types will be immediately recognizable and can serve as an internal model for the tendencies inherent in each type.

As noted previously, every individual is a blend of all seven types. While one may predominate, other types within us will respond in different situations. For example, we may be the aggressive Martial toward a subordinate and the withdrawn Lunar toward our boss; or we may be Lunar when we get out of bed and a Martial when someone cuts us off on the freeway.

In general, for all people, one set of tendencies will manifest most frequently and this will not be a pure type — such as Martial or Lunar — but a blended type, such as Lunar — Venusian. This blending, the circulation of types, follows the direction of the arrows in the Enneagram diagram. Most of the time, we'll manifest Mars-Jovial, Lunar-Venusian, Venusian-Mercury, Saturn-Mars, etc. Principally we respond or react first from our strongest or most habitual side. A Venusian-Mercury would be Venusian first then Mercury, a Saturn-Mars, Saturn first, then Mars and so on. We may also contain some Solar.

One more word of caution about type: a particular individual may not necessarily exemplify or manifest every characteristic of the type. For example, the Mercury type is manipulative and devious' yet a particular Mercury individual may be quite straightforward. Or he or she may be cunning on the job, yet act with Martial bluntness or Lunar introversion in the family. You might have a Mercury type who is not devious at all, because the essence — that which is individual about the person, is not devious, and in the individual's case, essence may be stronger than body type. In short, many individuals deviate from the type overall, but the type can still be seen in much of their behavior. For example, the Mercury's involvement in family affairs might be a passive, hidden form of deviousness, rather than an active attempt to circumvent others.

Body types are ultimately generalizations, but they are useful and powerful ones. Once observed, the presence of body type in a behavioral manifestations, whether it be yours or someone else's, is unmistakable. Overall it must be remembered that body types and the whole of Foundation Knowledge are alive, and by being such will exhibit both fixed and fluctuating characteristics.

Body Type & Social Conflict

The descriptions so far delineated are merely a starting ground for your own observations. The point is not to catalogue and dissect every possible characteristic of each body type, but rather to observe and verify that we do indeed behave according to influences beyond those presently known to us. *On The Elephant's Knee* is intended to serve as a reference sheet, a checklist of ideas which you can refer and connect to daily observations with Foundation Knowledge. Some of the ideas will be immediately verifiable, while others will take much longer, and in many cases, once the knowledge is sufficiently absorbed, it becomes possible to alter or correct weaknesses in one type by adding the strengths of another. This is also true for Center of Focus, Alchemy, and Chief Feature.

Interactions between types are specific and predictable. An understanding of these patterns can reduce disruptions, judgments and criticisms and provide for a greater possibility of harmonizing conflict.

For example, in stressful conditions, active and passive types clash. When the passive type gets upset, it shuts off, withdraws; whereas the active type expresses its stress, frustration or anger outwardly. The passive type gets cold, holds in anger, without expressing it; then, when it finally blows up, active types are shocked so they retaliate believing they are being unjustly accused. Then the passive type again gets cold and so on it goes.

Thus, Lunars take their time making decisions; Martials make immediate decisions. A Martial might be insisting that a Lunar decide something; for example, to go somewhere. The Martial says, "Come on let's go out. Do you want to go to a movie or dinner?" The Lunar has to think about this because it is passive and negative. The Lunar's first response is that they don't want to respond. And the second is that they're passive, so they're slow. The Martial becomes impatient with the Lunar's hesitation. The Lunar, in response, becomes more willfully withdrawn. The more insistent the Martial becomes, the more willful the Lunar becomes.

Or take the case of a recently married couple who quarreled after dinner. The fight concerned the husband's response to an unexpected, extended insult from one of their mutual friends. The husband, a gregarious, relaxed ex-fraternity member, listened to the diatribe for awhile and finally said, "Hey, ease-up." The wife fumed and sputtered, furious that her husband had not responded to the insult with an insult of his own. "Why didn't you defend yourself?" she complained. "I can't have my husband insulted in public!" "Honey," he said "It was no big deal." They went to bed angry, barely speaking, each blaming the other for an unreasonable position. They might have each understood and accepted the other's type. His easy-going, gregarious response was a classic Jovial's, her critical offense, the Mercurials. Neither was right nor wrong; neither's view of the situation represented an "objective" truth.

Take a job interview as another example. Let us say you are Mercurial, (perceptive, energetic, assertive) and you encounter a Martial (warlike, direct, and blunt). If you allow your Mercurial nature to dominate, you will likely excite a strong negative response. Mercuries and Martials are both active negative types, and tend to oppose one another. The slightest agitation from you will cause the Martial to respond in a warlike, aggressive fashion. The natural chemical reaction between the two of you is going to be confrontational. So you will want to play it cool, watching for signs of trouble.

Entire nations, races, neighborhoods, even species are also conditioned by the forces of Body Types. Sharks are Saturn-Mars fish, whales are Jovial and Jovial-Lunar, Dolphins-Solar, Piranhas-Martial, Shrimp are Mercury, Elephants are Jovial, Giraffes-Saturns, Lions-Martial, Monkeys-Mercury, Poodles are Mercury, St. Bernards-Jovial, German Shepherds-Saturn-Mars, Moles are Lunar, Cows-Venusian, the Irish Setter Solar-Saturn-Mars, Weeping Willow Trees are Venusian, Swamps are Venusian, Red Woods-Saturn, deserts-Martial, the Turks are Martial, the Chinese-Lunar, the Australians-Mars-Solar, Mexicans are Venusian-Mercury, etc.

Body type helps determine whether members of a group, be they marital partners, business executives, or players in a rock band, will be able to get along and work in harmony. For instance, George Bush, is a Lunar-Venusian type. Ronald Reagan, a Saturn-Mars, is his maximum attraction. They were drawn together. Bush was passive, practically nonexistent around Reagan.

In the Beatles, John Lennon was a Mercury-Saturn, Paul McCartney a Venusian-Mercury with a chief feature of vanity. Each of them expressed Mercury intelligence and perceptiveness in their music; however, the dominance and power of Lennon's Mercury-Saturn type was too demeaning for the vanity of McCartney's Mercury. Vanity automatically attracts attention, the effect of which causes him to expect more from himself because others expect more from him. This often leads people with vanity into a cycle of unhappiness sustained by the failure to satisfy expectations. And vanity tends to feel crushed by dominance and power because both can and do make things happen. People are entertained by vanity but are not moved by it. Moreover, as a Saturn, Lennon tended to be systematic and intellectual about his work. McCartney wanted most of all attention, the warmth of people, the adoration of fans. Lennon was respected, where McCartney was adored, but vanity is never satisfied. McCartney wanted respect, the respect people gave Lennon, from Lennon himself. But Saturnine dominance cannot respect as it is respected. It can be considerate, give praise and encouragement, congratulate, but not respect. Respect is for equals, and a Saturnine type with dominance concedes no equal.

Ringo Starr is a Lunar with a chief feature of Tramp, (A passive feature). He wasn't even a part of the show most of the

Venusian

Mercury

Saturn Mars

Mars Solar

Jovial Lunar

Mercury Saturn

Saturn

Martial

Mercury

Venusian

Jovial

Lunar

time in terms of a strong personality being brought to the audience. Ringo had to be pulled into the limelight; he was otherwise passive and withdrawn, typically Lunar. George Harrison was a Venusian, with a chief feature of non-existence. The passivity of Ringo and George helped keep the group together. There were no Martials in the band. Casting directors can use body type knowledge to assist their choice of actors and actresses. Let's say the casting director wants a strong, silent type: she'll want a Saturn. If she wants someone direct, blunt, and coarse, she'll want an instinctively-centered Martial. If she's looking for someone timid and soft, fragile and secretive, she'll be looking for Lunar. If she wants someone to play a part that is cheerful and naive, she'll want a Solar. If she wants someone with cunning, slyness, who looks like they can't be trusted even though they say "trust me," she'll want a Mercury. If she wants someone rotund and flamboyant, she'll seek a Jovial.

The ancients used body type to mate people, to coordinate social and family life, and to understand the enemy. We still have these needs today. Yet perhaps because there are too many answers, we live a more confused and disoriented life. Foundation Knowledge has value on many levels, the most practical being better human relations.

As a final note on body type, each type has positive and negative qualities. Indeed, any particular quality can be seen as either positive or negative, depending on the situation. For example, the Jovial's warmth can be experienced as either caring or smothering. Similarly, one can see a literal positive and negative side:

Lunar as cold or controlled under pressure
Venusian as lazy or contemplative
Mercury as devious or bright
Saturn as dominant or considerate

Martial as destructive or challenging
Solar as naive or refreshing

A Summary of the Seven Types:

Lunar	(cool, introspective, pale-skinned, willful, moody)
Venusian	(warm, sympathetic, thick-haired, pear-shaped, earthy)
Mercury	(bright, quick, cunning, perceptive)
Saturn	(tall, big-boned, stoic, dominating)
Martial	(aggressive, blunt, energetic, rough, reddish tone, destructive)
Jovial	(plump, giving, cheerful, colorful), and
Solar	(naive, fair, cheerful, frail).

The key is to observe these tendencies in yourself and in other people—to become aware of them. Once you are aware, you can decide whether to exaggerate the tendencies or begin to move outside of them, to see the tendencies as automatic reactions that occur within you, rather than as actions that you freely choose. As you see this, you begin to exercise greater understanding, choice, and more control over your manifestations; to act rather than react.

Tendency Chart #1 – Body Type

Type	Person	Place	Other Examples
SATURNINE or Saturn Mars	WILT CHAMBERLAIN KIM BASSINGER NICOLE KIDMAN FARRAH FAWCETT EMMA THOMPSON KAREEM ABDUL JABAR MICHAEL JORDAN PRINCESS DIANA ARNOLD SCHWARZENEGGER NICKE NOLTE BURT LANCASTER CANDACE BERGEN	ENGLAND WASHINGTON DC HIMALAYAS ARIZONA	REDWOOD PRAYING MANTIS GREAT DANE , EAGLE GIRAFFE, MOOSE GRANITE ROCKS
MARTIAL or Mars Jovial	MARGARET THATCHER JULIE ANDREWS RAMBO DAN QUAYLE PAUL NEWMAN BRAD PITT OLIVER NORTH JOHN MCENROE BORRIS BECKER MIKE TYSON BORIS YELTSEN BARBARA WALTERS HILLARY CLINTON MICHAEL J. FOX LUCILLE BALL DIONNE WARWICK	IRELAND ISTANBUL GERMANY	PIRANHA, LION, HAWK DESERTS, HAMMERS PIT BULLS, PRICKLY PEAR WALRUS, ELEPHANT ST. BERNARD
JOVIAL or Jovial Lunar	SANTA CLAUS JOHN GOODMAN ORSON WELLS BURL YVES SHELLEY WINTERS DALAI LAMA BRUCE WILLIS	FLAGSTAFF	WEDDINGS BARREL CACTUS ST. BERNARD, BUMBLEBEE PUFFER FISH, OWL PANDA, WATERMELON HIPPOS
LUNAR or Lunar Venusian	WOODY ALLEN STEVE MARTIN MEG RYAN CHEVY CHASE MELANIE GRIFFITH	GREENLAND RUSSIA CHINA	CHESS, POKER, MOLES DOVES BABY'S BREATH, KOALA, COTTONTAIL LAMB, POSSUM

Individual Body Types are usually a combination of two or three types which, in most cases, combine with
and can often be identified in any of the other types

Continued

Type	Person	Place	Other Examples
LUNAR or Lunar Venusian	OLIVIA HUSSEY JOHN MAJOR PAUL SIMON MEG TILLY JAMES SPADER GEORGE BUSH		 MOUSE
VENUSIAN or Venusian- Mercury	ELIZABETH TAYLOR SOPHIA LOREN FRANK SINATRA BURT REYNOLDS BARBARA HERSHEY SYLVESTER STALLONE FRANK SINATRA WARREN BEATTY JAY LENO DUSTIN HOFFMAN BARBRA STREISAND JOHN TRAVOLTA ROBIN WILLIAMS DELLA REESE ANTONIO BANDEROS ROBERT DI NERO ALEC BALDWIN SHIRLEY TEMPLE TOM CRUISE	BRAZIL NEW ORLEANS MEXICO ITALY SPAIN	BLOODHOUND WEEPING WILLOW SWAMPS, MOSS SEAL, COW GUINEA PIG, SLOTH ICE PLANT, ALGAE
MERCURIAL or Mercury Saturn	SAMMY DAVIS JR. JAMES WOODS JEFF GOLDBLUM JOHNNY CARSON EDDIE MURPHY WHITNEY HOUSTON NICHOLAS CAGE LEONARD NIMOY	PARIS FRANCE NEW YORK JAPAN	PING PONG JAYS, WASPS POODLE, FOX VENUS FLYTRAP SEA OTTER BIRDS OF PARADISE DOBERMAN PINCER CROW
SOLAR or Solar Planet Combinations	JULIA ROBERTS GOLDIE HAWN MICHAEL JACKSON SYDNEY POITIER JUDY GARLAND OLIVIA NEWTON JOHN HUGH GRANT	NETHERLANDS VENICE ITALY	DOLPHINS HUMMINGBIRDS WILD POPPY

ad of the primary or most obvious types except for the solar type which has no planetary affiliation

Tendency Chart #2 – Body Type

Type	Occupation
SATURN	BASKET BALL PLAYER, CROSS COUNTRY SKIER PRESIDENT, CEO, CHAIRMAN OF THE BOARD DIRECTOR, PRODUCER
MARS	POLICE OFFICER, FIREMAN, SALES, RUGBY PLAYER FOOTBALL, INFANTRYMAN
JOVIAL	BARTENDER, BUS DRIVER, CHEF, MATRE'D
LUNAR	CPA, DENTAL ASSISTANT, SECRETARY, BOOKKEEPER
VENUSIAN	NURSE, MASSEUSE, HOME ECONOMIST
MERCURY	LAWYER, CAR SALESMAN, REALTOR
SOLAR	ENTERTAINMENT COORDINATOR, DANCER WRITER, ARTIST

Tendency Chart #3 – Body Type

Body Types and their Typical Alchemy; Chief Feature and Center of Focus (apart from the individual)

Body Type	Typical Alchemy	Typical Feature	Typical Center
SATURN	GOLD	DOMINANCE	INTELLECTUAL
MARS	COPPER SILVER	DESTRUCTION/POWER	INSTINCTIVE/MOVING
JOVIAL	SILVER GOLD	POWER/VANITY	EMOTIONAL/INSTINCTIVE
LUNAR	SILVER GOLD	WILLFULNESS/LUNATIC	MOVING/INSTINCTIVE
VENUSIAN	SILVER	NON-EXISTENCE	INSTINCTIVE/EMOTIONAL
MERCURIAL	SILVER GOLD	POWER/VANITY	MOVING/INTELLECTUAL
SOLAR	SILVER GOLD	POWER/NAIVETE/VANITY	MOVING/INTELLECTUAL

Tendency Chart #4 – Body Type

Maximum Attraction Examples

Body Type	Alchemies	Features	Persons
Mars to Venusian	Like or one alchemy above or one alchemy below	Destructiveness to Non-existence	Nicole Kidman to Tom Cruise Alec Baldwin to Kim Bassinger Paul & Linda McCartney
Saturn to Lunar		Fear to Power	Prince Phillip to Queen Elizabeth II
Jovial to Mercury		Self pity to Non-existence	Bruce Willis to Demi Moore
Solar has no maximum attraction			

Tendency Chart #5 – Body Type

Maximum Repulsion Examples

Body Type	Alchemies	Features	Persons
Mars to Mercury	Alchemies more than one above or below	Power against power, dominance or willfulness	Mike Tyson against Robin Givens
Lunar to Mars	Gold against copper or lead	Vanity against self-pity	Stallone against Schwarzenegger
	Silver against lead		Queen Elizabeth against Eddie Murphy
	Copper against gold		Margaret Thatcher against Saddam Hussein
	Lead against silver or gold		Madonna against Sean Penn

Alchemy

Alchemy and Refinement

Alchemy refers to 'degree of refinement', refinement of thoughts, feelings, personal style, clothing, environment, etc. Both individuals and nations express alchemy, as do objects and places. A rusty car, torn overalls and slam dancing are less refined than a Rolls Royce, designer jeans and the waltz. A diamond ring more refined than a garbage can. There are four alchemies: Gold-Silver-Copper-Lead. Gold is the most refined, Lead the least refined.

In addition to refinement, alchemy may be viewed as the precision of an individual's aesthetic taste. Some would not even think of leaving the house without their three-hundred dollar Italian shoes; others might go to a meeting with a five-o-clock shadow. Some shrink from the smell of a bum on a crowded subway; others enjoy or tolerate the sweat, stench and crowds as a necessary component of travel. Again, the difference in alchemy may be grasped immediately by considering the extremes: New York's Upper East Side, on one hand, the Bowery the other; Princess Di on one hand, Madonna on the other.

Alchemy also may be viewed as the level or degree of one's tolerance for disorder. For example, a Vermeer painting celebrates the love of precision and order of an individual with a gold alchemy, while a Jackson Pollock, with its look of spaghetti plastered upon a naked canvas, will appeal to a person with copper or lead alchemy. Copper and lead alchemies,

Gold

Silver

Copper

Lead

because they lack the inherent and restrictive borders of silver and gold, have become fashionable in the West as a means for many to escape the rigors of maintaining silver and gold.

Lower alchemies are less concerned with maintenance: an invariable flow of attention is necessary to support a high level of refinement. Gold alchemy types, for example, will make a pair of shoes last for five years, in good condition, while someone with copper or lead alchemy will happily wear out the same pair of shoes over six months. Copper and lead alchemies figure that "things work until they don't then you fix them." Gold alchemies replace everything, or keep possessions in immaculate condition. They try to stay ahead of maintenance problems because they don't want to deal with the lack of or the absence of refinement. They'll have twenty rolls of toilet paper in their house instead of only one. Their car will be serviced a week ahead of time.

Personal hygiene is yet another way to assess alchemy. Gold alchemies will have clean or new clothes, take baths everyday, keep their nails clipped, their teeth brushed, their hair washed and combed. They will abhor smudges, dust, cracks, spills, detest disorder. With each alchemy moving away from gold, you will have less attention to hygiene. Someone with lead alchemy might think it is necessary to bathe only once a week. A copper alchemy might think every two or three days. Silver alchemy, every other day. Gold every day, or twice a day. Activities such as bathing, maintaining the home, washing dishes, vacuuming, the cleaning and pressing of clothes, having repairs made, buying new clothes as opposed to wearing old ones, all reflect alchemy.

The above are all different ways of exploring alchemy, much like seeing a sculpture from different angles. By observing the way a person looks, dresses, speaks, eats; the way he walks, says hello, reads, etc., we can see and verify alchemy. Alchemy encompasses speech, food, belief, dress, action, thought, and even emotions. Nearly all aspects of our lives are touched by alchemy, by a greater or lesser degree of refinement.

A gold alchemy tends to seek near perfection in appearance and habit; a silver alchemy is satisfied with slightly less; a copper alchemy tends to prefer slightly more disorder and finds the gold alchemy distasteful or pretentious; a lead alchemy affirmatively embodies disorder and lack of refinement.

The above categorization implies no value judgments. Like body type, each alchemy has its own unique advantages and disadvantages. Moreover, as with body type, our examples are somewhat exaggerated in order to demonstrate a pure alchemy. In reality, people's behavior will exhibit tendencies from more than one alchemy. The examples are not meant to state definitively that X person or Y person is or is not a Z alchemy. Rather, examples are designed to illustrate what is meant by gold, silver, copper or lead alchemy. Alchemy reflects a set of tendencies, rather than immutable "facts" or "problems" or "personality flaws." By observing alchemy, we can learn how to use these tendencies, rather than be trapped by them.

Identifying Alchemy

To identify alchemy, it is necessary to examine the level of refinement evident in one's behavior. We all wake up with tussled hair and morning breath, but an hour later, is every hair follicle neatly in place, the scarf tied in an Ascot knot, the shoes neatly polished, everything perfect and tidy and ready for inspection? If so, a gold alchemy is manifesting. The other three alchemies express correspondingly lesser degrees of this craving for refinement.

Thus, examining your preferences, from taste in art to choice of wallpaper, you can ask yourself:

-How extensive is my craving for refinement?

-How precise is my aesthetic sensibility?

-To what extent do I tolerate order?
-How much do I invest in appearance and environment?
-How scrupulous is my sense of personal hygiene?

On one level, we all have gold alchemy tendencies, in that we tend to judge beauty, as well as value, by their degree of refinement. We generally call lower alchemies ugly and valueless and higher alchemies beautiful, expensive, or invaluable. At the least, higher alchemy contributes to our perception of beauty and lower alchemy contributes to our perception of ugliness. Indeed, gold establishes the very notion of a hierarchy of refinement; it is because of the Hermes scarf, Rolex watch, and the Mercedes Benz, for instance, that we even think of objects and persons as having lower degrees of refinement. Gold is a competitive alchemy, and by its nature establishes comparisons and distinctions. As with type, exploring the concept of alchemy more fully allows us to appreciate differences in alchemy; to multiply our perspective rather than our being obligated to seeing the world through the alchemy we were born with and a singular one-dimensional perspective.

The Four Alchemies

GOLD

Gold represents the finest, or highest degree of refinement. Gold alchemy types like to dress, talk and present themselves in a more precise or refined way. That does not make them better than other people, but they see themselves as obligated to be more attentive or refined than others. People with a gold alchemy are generally fair. Their skin tone, hair color, and choice of clothes are light, delicate and fine. Their features make them appear sharp – as if more in focus – than other people with another alchemy.

Gold

Because gold alchemies seek ultimate refinement in themselves, they tend to be highly alert to refinement in others.
When they walk into your home, for example, gold alchemies
immediately notice the Waterford crystal, the Scandinavian
furniture, the diamond and gold watch on your wrist, the
Hermes scarves in your wardrobe. (If you lack these, the gold
alchemy will notice as well.)

Gold alchemy types are often impractical people because
they tend to take refinement too far. For example, a gold
alchemy person may wish that every item on the coffee table
always be in exactly the same place, perfectly arranged, every
window without a spot, each word perfectly uttered. They'll
resent mistakes, because mistakes are sloppy. They want
clothes perfectly ironed and well maintained.

The "need" for refinement can and often does supersede
good judgment. Choices which make perfect sense to gold

alchemy, often seem tiresome and impractical to family members, spouse, friends and professional acquaintances with silver or copper alchemies. For instance, someone with a gold alchemy may want a new pair of shoes for every occasion. To silver alchemy, who is more conservative, practical or more functional with regard to the necessities of life, spending money on shoes for every occasion will appear quite extreme.

In the office, individuals with a gold alchemy tend to have their shoes polished every morning, or at least every couple of days. Whether or not they can afford the latest style their shoes will always appear shiny and new. Someone with a silver, copper or lead alchemy will wait longer before polishing those shoes, getting that haircut, tucking in that shirttail, buying that new coat, throwing out the tie that is beginning to fray at the edges.

The kind of work or activities gold alchemies prefer are often less strenuous. They don't get involved in "heavy duty" activities such as trash collection. They dislike soiling their hands. They want to associate with cleaner, more refined material. A gold alchemy will be attracted to jobs with little or no manual labor. Manual labor produces sweat. It makes you dirty. Someone with a gold alchemy will avoid manual work. A gold alchemy will be found in an air-conditioned office, his sleeves rolled down, gold cufflinks and tie-pin accenting lines of a fine 100% cotton shirt.

Moreover, the gold alchemy will focus on the fact that manual labor produces a strong physical smell. The smell is seen as "disgusting," offensive, even frightening, rather than as a natural biological emanation. The people who produce it are considered "dirty" and are seen as "deserving" their low economic status. This is not to say that you will never have people of gold alchemy in jobs involving manual labor. Economic and life circumstances create all kinds of conditions. However, people with a gold alchemy will tend to prefer activ ities that require less manual labor, less physical involvement. They will become hospital administrators rather than emergency room surgeons, corporate lawyers rather than legal aid society lawyers, engineers rather than plumbers, designers of cars rather than auto mechanics.

Just as individuals reflect the various alchemies, so do cities, countries, even particular jobs and industries. For example, the film industry overall is a gold alchemy industry; the technological refinements involved in making a film are very high. Moreover, film-making attracts many people with a gold alchemy. It also encompasses jobs that copper and lead alchemy people don't mind doing, such as sanitation, catering, and printing press work.

EXAMPLES: Movie stars often convey alchemy in their roles. For instance, Sean Connery, a gold alchemy, appears proper or refined even when he is getting killed. His acting routine is neither careless nor haphazard, but carries an air of order and precision, a pre-programmed instinct to behave in a refined manner. Connery's characters like fine cigarettes, fine wines, fine women.

Michelle Pfeiffer has a gold alchemy. She appears sophisticated even in tough roles. They way she moves her hands, the postures she takes, the sharpness of her body, all exhibit the attention to detail that exemplifies gold alchemy people. By way of contrast, Elizabeth Taylor has a silver alchemy. She is elegant but not refined. Her choice of clothing and jewelry serves the practical purpose of reminding everyone who she is and what she has accomplished. A gold alchemy like Mia Farrow will buy expressly for the refined quality of a particular dress, specific ring, necklace or antique. Taylor, like Zsa Zsa Gabor, is slightly gaudy in appearance, whereas Faye Dunaway, Mia Farrow, Michelle Pfeiffer and Julia Roberts are clearly natural in refined settings. Again, alchemy is not a measure of character, but of one's sense of refinement. Nonetheless, alchemy affects one's image and appearance. When a silver alchemy person tries to be a gold alchemy person, it shows – you can tell they're "acting."

Charleton Heston, Sidney Poitier, Kevin Costner, and Brat Pitt all have gold alchemy. Refinement on these men appears natural, believable. They are tidy, from their speech, to their dress, to the way they sit. There is always something slightly off or awkward about the way that silver – copper, and lead alchemy actors act the part of a gold alchemy character. Similarly, gold alchemies have difficulty playing roles that do not accommodate their alchemy.

Queen Elizabeth and Princess Diana each has a gold alchemy, while Charles has a silver alchemy. His brother Andrew has a gold alchemy, Fergie has a silver copper alchemy. Queen Elizabeth's husband has a gold alchemy. Princess Ann has a gold alchemy. Royalty are programmed to exhibit a gold alchemy. The whole physiology of royalty is the finest of everything. In England, people are referred to as having a pure or tainted pedigree; Americans (or those not of royal descent) are considered mutts, mongrels. The Royal Family is supposed to be the height of purity. Even if an individual member is born with a lead alchemy (which is unlikely because they have generations of breeding gold alchemy people), they would act like a gold alchemy and strive to marry someone with a gold alchemy.

Whitney Houston has a gold alchemy. Eddie Murphy has a gold alchemy, although his humor is often copper-lead. The gold alchemy is evident in his refined stylishness, his upper crust demeanor, the copper-lead in his predilection for swearing. The contradiction between Murphy's alchemy and his choice of words may be part of what makes him humorous. The gold alchemy of Whitney Houston, Diana Ross and Vanessa Williams, as with all gold alchemy people, can be seen in the way they present themselves; the way they walk, talk, dress, and so on.

All we need to do to verify alchemy is to observe consistent differences between people's approaches to refinement. For instance, with Meryl Streep, when you look at her characters, and at the way in which she presents herself when she is interviewed, you will find an air of refinement. This air is important to her, and to gold alchemy people in general. Gold alchemies have difficulty playing roles that do not accommodate their alchemy.

IN RELATIONSHIPS: In relationships, gold alchemies can be too fussy about the environment, about details, propriety, appearances, presentation. They can be rigid in exercising their need for refinement in the environment. Gold alchemies tend to be intolerant; at times, the need for order and refinement overrides feelings of tenderness and nurturing. Gold is the least forgiving of the alchemies. You don't want to make mistakes with gold alchemies, because a mistake is an act of unrefinement, which to gold is a crime.

Gold alchemies tend to be stingy, while copper and lead alchemies tend to be generous, both financially and emotionally. Even though gold alchemies are on the whole wealthier, they are generally less giving.

IN SOCIETY: Gold alchemies tend to set the standards of society. For example, gold alchemies have established the standard for religion in the West; our society typically equates spirituality with refinement. The Catholic religion typifies the gold alchemy. Everything in the religion is embellished with gold alchemy qualities: the Vatican, with its marbled halls and art masterpieces; the concept of Immaculate Conception (what could be more refined than conception without sex); the notion that certain prayers must be said on certain days and in specific order. Everything must be in its place, functioning correctly and in order — even the vision of Christ in his sandals represents a refinement of spirit. One could argue that the Church, in fact, has gotten so much into the display of refinement that refinement itself tends to stand for religious feeling. One is lead to feel that one cannot have a religious feeling without refinement.

We can see that in Catholicism, as one example, the service, the rites, and the very structure of worship the church reflects the bias toward a high degree of refinement. The motto is, "cleanliness is next to godliness." By way of contrast in some ancient cultures, cleanliness is as completely irrele vant to the concept of spiritual awakening; and one could argue that physical or material refinement has little or nothing to do with spirituality.

The clash in alchemies naturally explains conflicts within religious organizations dominated by their alchemy. Thus, the spiritual leaders of a gold alchemy institution will attempt to crush the intrusion of other alchemies into their worship. For instance, the Church was scandalized when St. Francis brought animals into worship, and wandered as a beggar from town to town – a strong dose of copper-lead alchemical ten dencies. Since his time, soup kitchens for the homeless have become a part of the religious institution. Soup kitchens now are accepted in the religious culture – so long as they remain in the back of the church, and not inside of it. Gold alchemy is quick to ostracize any failure of reverence. In a gold alche my home people are ruled by the home itself not by the own ers as the owners too must bow to the alchemy.

Again, since the notion of alchemy is complex enough to embrace every facet of our lives, we can see a variety of alchemies being expressed within any dominant structure including, to complete the example above, the Catholic reli gion. For instance, the bloody crucifix, the notion of physical sacrifice, along with the focus on the Crucifixion, manifest copper and lead alchemy. The protestant crucifix, in contrast which lacks the corpus of Jesus, manifests a silver-gold alchemy, with its clean, sharp lines and geometric unity.

Many large corporations display a gold alchemy, with their rich offices, plush carpeting and expensive decor. Indeed, gold alchemy in the West is regularly equated with success. This is because gold alchemy in a physical sense means, "the best"; the best wine, the best cars. If you're living in the eighteenth century, the best horse and carriage; the best knight and the best gown, the best silk and lace. Harvard and Yale are gold alchemy institutions. Gold alchemy homes, offices and institutions are given more value than the people in them. Gold alchemy, as an institution, does not suggest behavioral norms, it dictates them.

SILVER

Silver alchemies are practical in their dress, their friendships, living environment, and job choices. They share the gold alchemy's taste for a high degree of refinement, but generally will demand (and accept) a lesser degree, and one that is tempered by practical concerns. For instance, a gold alchemy would buy shoes that are highly refined but unlikely to last, while a silver alchemy will buy a pair of shoes that might not be as refined – but will be solid and durable, and perhaps a bit klunkier.

Silver alchemies choose colors that are practical, often more subdued, darker colors, which last longer and hide the dirt. They tend to have dark hair, though not necessarily dark eyes, and a darker than average complexion.

EXAMPLES: The English have a silver alchemy as a country. They are often very conservative in their dress and behavior. Their taste for refinement is moderated by practicality. For instance, they will purchase a washing machine, and keep on repairing it rather than buying a new one.

The silver alchemy's practicality goes into keeping things

Silver

working. It is not the same maintenance as a gold alchemy, who maintains products and possessions simply for the sake of aesthetic beauty; the silver's concept of maintenance is to keep things working. Silver alchemies aren't fussy about how things look, so long as they work.

IN SOCIETY: Since appearance has a lot to do with the expression of alchemy, a silver alchemy will be well-dressed but not as tight and tidy as a gold alchemy. The gold alchemy will go out for a drink in a Brooks Brother's suit; the silver alchemy may wear a blazer; the copper will be casually dressed; the lead will wear torn jeans, ripped at the knee. The professor wearing the corduroy jacket with the elbow patch is expressing a silver alchemy, while his son with the ragged T-shirt is expressing a copper or lead alchemy.

COPPER

Copper alchemies like the coarse, rough life, the hard sound, the tough look. Copper and lead alchemies tend to be less punctual than gold and silver, and enjoy things that are durable and entirely functional; beauty is irrelevant.

In general, the greater the population, the more intense the pressure to survive, and the lower the alchemy. As global population increases, the planet's alchemy as a whole plummets and with it "quality of life."

EXAMPLES: When Mickey Rourke gets dirty, he's really dirty. Gold alchemy actors such as Paul Newman and Robert Redford may fall in the dirt, but somehow they don't look dirty, you don't feel the dirt embedded in them. Gold alchemy people have trouble retaining such a look. If the part requires them to fall in the mud, they do so but we know the mess is only on the surface. When copper is dirty, it is dirty to

Copper

the bone.   Mickey Rourke has a copper-sliver alchemy. Madonna has a copper-silver alchemy.

The Hell's Angels are primarily a copper-lead organization, when one considers their appearance and lifestyle. By way of contrast, Greenpeace and the Sierra Club people are gold-silver alchemy organizations; they strive to maintain the high quality of nature's beauty and function.

IN SOCIETY: Much of our age expresses a copper alchemy in conjunction or collaboration with the chief feature of tramp: a loss of the disciplines which support responsible self-evaluation. Wearing clothes that are torn to pieces and presenting yourself as excessively tolerant, disheveled, unkempt, and un-cared for is a tendency of the chief feature of tramp. Copper alchemy is very comfortable with that kind of disheveled, disorderly look. It doesn't mind having tears in its clothes, tattoos, punctured skin, or having furniture that barely holds up. It doesn't mind going to the edge of maintenance, or disregarding maintenance altogether.

Copper and lead alchemy are fashionable these days: the punk fad, destruction of the body with drugs, the worn and torn look in jeans, the disharmony in art and music. These are less refined elements of our lives, yet attract many individuals, since these alchemies, in lacking clear and defined boundaries, appear, mistakenly, to offer greater freedom of self-expression. Copper and lead alchemies are not easily angered by problems with material existence and the environment. They may think nothing of tossing a lunch bag full of garbage out of a moving car, or spilling wine on a carpet in their own home. Most pollution, however, comes from those in the industrialized gold-alchemy nations, who have sacrificed the well-being of the whole for the sake of individual refinement, and greed.

Copper alchemy people often have a copper or "golden" skin tone. And it can be difficult, with a well bread copper alchemy person, to distinguish between gold and copper alchemies by first appearance. Both may have lighter colored hair and fine clothes. Copper alchemies will express a greater coarseness however or lack of preference for refinement overall, and often may have a more guttural or less precisely articulated speaking voice.

Copper alchemies don't mind spitting or urinating on the street. Similarly, a lead alchemy will do the same yet more openly. Copper and lead alchemies don't mind grotesque exposure or exposing the instinctive digestive functions of the body. Burping, swearing, and releasing gas in public are copper-lead behaviors.

LEAD

Lead is the least refined alchemy. There are fewer lead alchemies in the West than in the East, parts of Africa and South America. The most abundant alchemies in the West are silver and copper. The same goes for our global population overall, although there are probably more silver alchemies than any other kind of alchemy. After silver, we have equal proportions of copper and gold and relatively few of the lead. The lead alchemies we do find in the West have jobs such as working in sanitation, garbage collection, slaughter houses, the back rooms of run down restaurants and bars, dish washing. Unrefined manual labor attracts lead alchemies.

EXAMPLES: Drug addiction manifests the lead alchemy's penchant for a low regard for the maintenance of and refinement of the body. Abuse of the body, whether one has a lead alchemy or not, is a manifestation of lead alchemy.

On the Indian subcontinent the caste once known as "Untouchables" manifests the concept of lead alchemy. Describing a group of people or an activity manifesting lead alchemy is to describe a condition, not a preference or character choice. Thus, poverty often manifests lead alchemy, while

Lead

owning a B.M.W. manifests gold. An individual with a gold alchemy may find himself born as a beggar, with the necessity of living in a lead environment. And a lead alchemy could be born into England's Royal family.

Neither alchemy nor any other Foundation Knowledge concept is presented here to justify or to perpetuate racism, sexism, elitism, injustice, etc. Our purpose is to uncover truth not subvert it. India's lower castes, America's homeless, drug abuse, terrorism and wars, African famine, economic under-development, inept government policies all reflect a global manifestation of chief features warped relationship to alchemy which has forced millions of individuals into a life of lead even if their individual alchemy is otherwise.

IN SOCIETY: One of the positive aspects of lead alchemy is tolerance. Lead alchemy people require very little to feel satisfied and content. Lead alchemy is the most flexible alchemy, the most relaxed while gold is the most intolerant. Lead alchemy people tend to be generous and forgiving. Their environment may not be attractive but they are often pleasant to be with; typically, the reverse is true of the gold alchemies. They might dwell in a beautiful environment, yet act bitchy, fussy, unhappy if things don't go well. They may scream and yell over the tiniest scratch, error or bump, acting as if the world had just ended. Gold alchemies often appear highly neurotic and indeed most people under the care of therapists, psychologists, and psychiatrists are gold alchemy people. Alchemy thus reveals a paradox of the human condition; the environment of a gold alchemy person is clean, attractive, beautiful and refined but the person within may be unpleasant. On the other hand, the lead alchemies who are frequently warm, generous, will give strangers food, shelter and clothing, whatever hospitality they can offer, even though they are living in a dump. We find ourselves attracted to gold alchemies on one hand, and lead alchemies on another. Alchemy is always a mixed bag. We never seem to have everything one way – there is always this combination as in maximum attraction with body types.

Again, the principles of alchemy refer to tendencies – behavior patterns in which individuals are most comfortable. Often, when people learn about alchemy, nobody wants to be described as lead or copper. This is natural, as we all wish the best for ourselves and it sounds, initially, like gold is better than lead. But alchemy does not make the individual. It does not, cannot, establish good character. As with body type, alchemy is part of what we are, not our totality and not fixed.

With our four vehicles we have a clear visual example of how alchemies can be discerned. The gold alchemy car has a high level of refinement of design, functions and materials. All new cars are not gold alchemy however. A new Volkswagon for example, is a silver alchemy car which can through time, if it is not maintained, degrade to copper, then lead. Most new cars are silver alchemy with many indigenous third world cars often being copper. Maintenance sustains the original alchemy of a car, object, house, etc. But it does not change an alchemy. Neglect, abuse, and disregard lowers alchemy. Creativity and invention can raise alchemy.

With Knowledge the choice is ours, we can choose to shape our alchemy or we can choose to do nothing.

Alchemy and Family

Many domestic quarrels emerge from a simple clash in alchemy, rather than reflecting any deeper moral or substantive issue. For example, a gold alchemy will have trouble living in any environment that is messy, dirty, or simply disorganized. That is a given with the gold alchemy. The silver, copper and lead do not mind a bit of mess; the gold will insist on scrupulous order.

Let's say a man buys an endless assortment of ties, satisfying his gold alchemy. He feels perfectly justified about this expenditure. His wife, who has a copper or lead alchemy, is looking "practically" at the expenditure. She says: "We can't afford donating such a large portion of our income to your wardrobe." He replies: "I have to make a good impression at the office." Each one will expect the other to see the "logic" of his or her position. Yet, the position is not driven by logic, but by alchemy. He sees extreme refinement in dress as a requirement for work; her aesthetic sense is tempered by budgetary concerns. He will be buying the Hermes ties, at a hundred dollars a piece; she will prefer a greater variety of less expensive design.

Alchemy, of course, cannot and should not be used as a source for judgment or to excuse bad behavior. For instance, a parent complains to the child about the child's habits: Parent: "Why don't you clean your room more often? Put away your toys and clothes; this place looks like a pigsty!" Child: "It's my lead alchemy. And if yours wasn't gold, you wouldn't care."

On the other hand, if the parent knew that the child had a copper alchemy or a lead alchemy – as a result of which the child would naturally tend to be disorderly or messy, the parent would tend to be more forgiving of the child and the child less critical of the parent. It is easy to find something wrong with another person's behavior, but to be critical and negative about inherent differences produces much unnecessary suffering.

Knowledge of alchemy might also be used to change the child's habits. If the child is made to understand that his or her way is to be disorganized and dirty – that this is a built-in characteristic, a matter of alchemy – then the child will consider disorganization a tendency rather than an unshakable necessity. There will be no shame. The disorganization will not be considered the child's fault, but a tendency he was born with, one he can alter. Knowing his alchemy, he has a choice of direction; he can feel some control, a chance to do something about his manifestations.

Silver alchemy children of gold alchemy parents are never going to be clean enough, tidy enough, dressed nicely enough, behave well enough and so on because the parents will be addicted to refinement. If there is no understanding within the family, then behavioral patterns (for example, keeping the room messy) are misunderstood as deliberate manifestations of argument or rebellion. And this misunderstanding will habituate and cause the child, in his later life, to strike out against authority figures who demand that he act against his alchemy.

Alchemy and National Identity

Different nations, races and cultures have different alchemies. The French have a gold alchemy. They have an extreme sense of refinement, especially with regard to the French language. If it's not pure French being spoken the French won't listen. The Italians, in contrast, have little trouble with badly spoken Italian. The Italians have a silver-gold alchemy and they're emotionally centered. Communication is more important than refinement to an emotionally centered type.

Within France, different regions have different alchemies. Paris has a gold alchemy: Parisian fashions and perfumes are among the very finest in the world. (Fashion and perfume are in themselves gold alchemy concepts.)

Germans have, in a sense, a heavy gold alchemy. They want refinement but it has to be strong. For them, refinement means making something equally strong and beautiful. They have a lot of the Martial type in them, so refinement must not mean a loss of strength. The Mercedes is a good example. In fact, most durable luxury cars come out of Germany. Similarly, some of the best machine tools are German.

The Spanish have a silver alchemy: they tend to be relaxed, although passionate; they like to have things refined to the level of comfort. The ancient Greeks were gold, but today's Athens is a copper alchemy city, a basic city, an almost purely functional city. In general, as long as their basic needs are taken care of, today's Greeks are happy.

The Italians believe you work to live, not live to work. The Americans are always trying to work themselves to death. This is more a difference in body type than one of alchemy, yet alchemy does play a role here, as most Americans work to acquire a more refined standard of living. Italians work to spend time with their children, to enjoy family and friends, to enjoy life for emotional reasons, which is, in fact, an expression of gold alchemy in the emotional center, a refinement of feelings.

The United States as a whole has a gold-silver alchemy. Some parts of a country will be more gold (Boston, for example), others more silver (say, Ohio), others lead (say, Appalachia).

All cities, towns and villages have an alchemy. People will settle in different geographical regions depending in part on their alchemy. People with gold alchemy, for instance, would be comfortable in countries like Switzerland or Sweden, which have gold alchemies, or cities like Paris or San Francisco, which have a gold or silver-gold alchemy.

One can sense alchemy in refinement of the city and the attitude of its people. Munich, Rome, Paris and Venice have gold alchemies, while London has a silver-gold alchemy. Edinburgh has a silver alchemy. Copper alchemy cities include Athens and Calcutta. New Delhi is primarily copper, with silver and lead equally, and traces of gold. New Orleans is silver-gold. New York has a silver-gold alchemy overall, though a neighborhood like Soho would be copper-silver. The Upper East Side is gold, while the Upper West Side is silver; Harlem is copper or lead. Wall Street has a gold alchemy.

Overall, Western Europe has a silver-gold alchemy. India, in contrast, has a copper-lead alchemy. Many Westerners have difficulty understanding and appreciating India because of its alchemy. Westerners are taught that you can not have an awakening or an elevating experience in an impoverished, unsanitary situation. This is, of course, untrue. Indeed, lead or copper alchemy can allow more openness to the religious experience, since lead is the most generous and most forgiving of the alchemies, and lead has the greatest amount of emotional flexibility.

Animals, bugs, cars, guns, jewelry, birds, toys – everything has an alchemy. The Rover, for example, is a gold alchemy 4x4: beautiful and sleek, yet still a reliable drive. Old, beat-up jeeps have a copper alchemy: they are purely functional vehicles. You have your lead alchemy clunkers and your gold alchemy Roll Royces and limousines. Fabrics have different alchemies, to the extent they are more refined or more coarse. Silk, for example, is a gold alchemy fabric, wool is silver-copper, cotton is silver-gold.

Refinement and attention to detail, concern about detail, concern about refinement. This is Alchemy. Thus, individuals most concerned about refinement and detail often have a gold alchemy. However, a person with a chief feature of lunatic or vanity can also be overly concerned with refinement. The concept of alchemy is a guide, not a foolproof method for typing. Sometimes you will receive mixed messages in trying to determine one's alchemy. The more you begin to employ the information, the easier it will become to identify what is, for instance, a gold alchemy versus a pronounced characteristic of a Solar body type or a chief feature of vanity. By using a process of elimination you can arrive at a final conclusion of whether or not your evaluation is an alchemical one.

Alchemy and Social Attitudes

Racial conflicts often stem from differences in alchemy. Depending on one's perspective, some kinds of people are considered "dirty," others "snooty," still others, "unsophisticated," and so on. Some like themselves with perfume, others bathe infrequently. Each regards the other as inferior, but in fact as a result of their alchemies, they tend to have different kinds of living conditions and modes of appreciation. And that difference is too often equated as something negative, even confrontational, rather than simply a difference resulting from alchemy.

For example, in America, whites often have a higher alchemy than blacks, creating, an often unconscious and false sense of superiority in whites and inferiority in blacks. Similarly, upper-class whites and blacks have a higher alchemy than many in the lower-class, which again creates a false perception of superiority and inferiority. To make matters worse, gold alchemies exaggerate their wealth, show off their status with displays of refinement, which irritates the lower alchemies. In being too often ostentatious with their jewelry, fancy homes, and cars, they evoke in the lower alchemies a desire to accumulate similar possessions, in order to prove that they are just as good. But alchemy is not the man. Few people realize this.

As was mentioned earlier, drug addiction reflects a lead alchemy, an unrefined approach to the body, and it's often associated with alchemically weak conditions, such as begging on the street and homelessness. However, in the West, social disgust reflects the chagrin experienced by gold or silver alchemies when faced with an unrefined situation more than discomfort over the plight of the needy. The fact that people are mentally ill or addicted to drugs upsets the conscience less than the fact that these people are unrefined, dirty things which infringe upon a perfect world. This is not to say that citizens are not genuinely concerned with the problem of homelessness or drug abuse, but to suggest that alchemical preferences play an important part in one's political and social perspective. On the whole, gold alchemies are more concerned with heroin addicts in Harlem and Amsterdam than they are with the Wall Street banker who makes a million dollars a year and does crack between board meetings.

Alchemical tendencies are not fixed, you or I can raise or lower our alchemy. (If you live in certain parts of Russia, you will be forced to lower your alchemy. In Monaco, you will raise it – if you can afford to.) Countries can change over time. Ancient Greece had a gold alchemy, now Greece has copper-lead alchemy. That fine line drawn by perception between what is and is not socially and publicly acceptable is the concept of alchemy.

Esoterically, the purpose of studying alchemy is to become more aware of spiritual possibilities; more aware of how much we have to learn; more capable of achieving the highest level of refinement of the body: the awakening in us of the state of non-participating observation. When the alchemists spoke of transforming lead into gold, they did not mean metallic changes, but the transformation of physical man: coarse matter into spirit. Achieving gold represented the success of pilgrimage from mortality to immortality. According to the ancients; we are not born with a guaranteed afterlife identity, only the potential for one. Immortality must be earned and created much like a mother labors to give birth to a child.

Alchemy and Character

Alchemy is, to some extent, inherited from one's family. Most children have either one or the other or a combination of the alchemies of their parents. For instance, a person whose father has a gold alchemy and whose mother has a silver alchemy will likely have a gold alchemy, a silver alchemy, or a silver-gold alchemy. It is unusual for a child to have an alchemy completely different than that of either one of the parents.

Generally, the higher the alchemy, the more exploitive the individual. Gold alchemy tends to produce an insatiable desire for more and more refinement, which in some individuals becomes corrupt as they lose sight of other people, and intensify the acquisition of more refined clothes, cars, homes, jewelry, and other objects.

Like body type, no alchemy is "superior" or "inferior" to another; all are equally mechanical, equally bound to mortality. A gold alchemy person might think himself superior to someone with a silver alchemy (or the reverse may occur), but this is simply distorted thinking. Someone with lead alchemy doesn't have an advantage or disadvantage over someone with gold or silver alchemy. All are equally in need of further refinement, greater spiritual awakening.

Someone with lead alchemy can evolve, can become more conscious, more spiritual just as well as someone with gold. A Mercurial can achieve nirvana as readily as a Jovial, Solar or Saturn. An emotionally centered type as well as an instinctive type. Alchemy represents an imbalance, a tendency to choose one food when there are four available. And this tendency is given, not earned; it is born in us. To evolve, to impassion our lives with harmony, thankfulness, the joy of learning; to become fully human, to awaken, we must learn to balance our alchemical tastes to balance our types, centers of focus, and our chief features to "realize" our inherent right to an evolving perspective.

Tendency Chart #6 – Alchemy

Alchemical Possibilities

Gold   **Silver**   Copper   **Lead**

Most individuals have combined alchemies as illustrated below.

Gold Silver	Silver Copper	Copper Lead
Silver Gold	Copper Silver	Lead Copper

Tendency Chart #7 – Alchemy

Alchemical Compatibility

	Gold	Silver Gold	Silver	Copper Silver	Copper	Lead Copper	Lead
Gold	Y	Y	Y	S	N	N	N
Silver Gold	Y	Y	Y	S	N	N	N
Silver	Y	Y	Y	Y	Y	S	N
Copper Silver	N	S	Y	Y	Y	S	N
Copper	N	N	Y	Y	Y	Y	Y
Lead Copper	N	N	S	S	Y	Y	Y
Lead	N	N	N	S	Y	Y	Y

Y = Yes   N = No   S = Strained

112

Tendency Chart #8 – Alchemy

Alchemies	Person	Other Examples
Gold	Princess Diana Robert Redford Linda McCartney David Niven Michelle Pfeiffer Whitney Houston Sydney Poitier Paul Newman Brad Pitt	Paris. Switzerland San Francisco Venice, Italy Irish Setter, Rose Collie, Jaguar
Silver Gold	Robert Dinro Nick Nolte Michael J. Fox Shelley Winters Meg Tilly	New Orleans, BMW
Silver	Zsa Zsa Gabor Dustin Hoffman Prince Charles Elizabeth Taylor Burt Reynolds Robin Williams	London, England Frankfurt, Oak Trees Mules, Honda
Copper Silver	Christian Slater Woody Allen	Lisbon, Volkswagon
Copper	Madonna Mickey Rourke Mike Tyson	Athens, Bombay Greece, India Crabgrass, Lions, Chevy Vega
Lead Copper		Tijuana, Old ATV
Lead		Bangledesh, Calcutta The Bowery. Slums Mud, Pigs Clunker Cars

Chief Feature

Chief feature refers to a person's principal weakness or vice; his chief fault or "original sin"; that place in us where we choose between the development of powers or being; where we choose to attach ourselves more firmly to a one dimensional material realty or free ourselves from it. Chief feature is primarily an energy source, which, prior to the establishment of intent, is neutral. For example, a gun is neutral whether we use it to hunt food to feed our family or to murder somebody. The choice we make reveals intent. If the intent is evil then the chief feature is evil. If the intent is benevolent then the chief feature is benevolent.

Each of us falls, despite our best intentions, into situations that are detrimental to ourselves and other people. The weakness behind this fall is chief feature. Chief feature, in conjunction with the negative half of the intellectual part of the instinctive center, represents the dark side of the soul; a parasitic intelligence, often invisible to us, which seeks to manipulate to our advantage the weaknesses in other people.

Chief feature works behind our backs in ways that appear to be to our benefit, but in fact are as unkind toward us as toward others. Chief feature aims at acquiring only for itself from everyone we meet, from every situation. Chief feature does not give; it takes. Being ruthless and selfish, chief feature cares only about itself.

There are at least twelve categories of chief feature: power, vanity, greed, self-pity, destructiveness, dominance, fear, lunatic, tramp, willfulness, naivete, and non-existence. Some of these have been identified as Christianity's "seven deadly sins". Others have been mapped in various systems as principal defenses or neurosis. For instance, vanity might be identified with narcissism. While Christian lore and psychoanalytic systems consider the feature to be an aspect of the individual, Foundation Knowledge implies that the feature has a life of its own. The personality of every individual is subjugated to chief feature, rather than the reverse. Thus, Christian spirituality aims at "rooting out" the deadly vice; psychoanalysis aims at separating the person from the symptom, and giving the individual a measure of control. Foundation Knowledge illuminates how an entire personality can pivot around chief feature. According to the Knowledge, it is not the individual who is expressing the chief feature, rather it's the chief feature which is expressing itself through the individual.

Like body type and alchemy, chief feature is an archetypal form of energy: a law, one that uses human beings to express itself. Thus, it is not that "I" have a problem with greed, but rather "greed" that has a use for me. In other words, there is an actual energy or entity of greed, one that feeds off something in men who are attracted to greed. Our job; our principle interest concerning chief feature is not to subdue the manifestations of power, greed, vanity, etc., but to gain control over the often selfish and vindictive intentions behind the manifestations. Intention can be changed, made to serve rather than to subjugate.

Each individual will have within himself elements of all the features. However, one feature, our 'Chief Feature', will dominate. In short, we are not exploring the presence or absence of each feature in a person, rather the degree. Nobody is completely free of, fear, vanity, or destructiveness. Thus, we cannot hope to totally remove chief feature. What we can do is to observe, and by observation distract chief feature through developing the positive qualities of the other features which have less control over us. Chief feature is neutral in us until the establishment of intent. In addition, every feature has a cycle of influence; a period of time that it prospers. In many cases the feature can exhaust itself or become saturated. When this occurs it tends to move towards the next strongest feature in a person or society. For example; a person or society with Tramp feature, once it saturates, has a tendency to move towards lunatic or greed.

Power may move towards Destructiveness or Greed. The tendency would be for power to move towards self-destruction once it realizes it cannot become any more powerful, once it saturates or perceives a limitation to power. The inclination would be for it to destroy what it created. A good example of this transition is the fall of the Roman Empire. Another example of Primary feature to Secondary feature would be Greed to Self-Pity, not being able to get any greedier. Ah, I can't have anymore; I think I'll feel sorry for myself.

Identifying Chief Feature

A good place to look for chief feature is where you make decisions, particularly difficult ones. Studying your decisions regarding where to live, who to live with, what kind of job to take, whether or not to have children, where you want to go for vacation, you can ask; where is chief feature behind these choices? Who is the enemy? Who is the friend?

For example, suppose you graduate college and decide to work in the film industry. Each chief feature will seek a position in the film industry most comfortable for it, not you. The position of director, for instance, will often attract individuals with a chief feature of dominance or power. Because being a director gives one maximum amount of power and influence over the audience, and over others in the industry.

Individuals with a chief feature of vanity, on the other hand, will be drawn to being actors. A vanity feature desires attention. Of all positions in the industry, acting offers the greatest possibility for attention since the actor is "on stage" feeding off the attention nearly all the time. In a similar vein, the position of producer will attract those with a chief feature of greed. This is not to say that actors and directors cannot be "greedy" but merely that the allure of "making a killing" is more easily satisfied in the position of producer than in that of an actor or director, while the need for attention is most easily satisfied in the actor's role, and the hunger for dominance in the director's.

The following chart lists the twelve chief features, describes whether the feature is active (A) or passive (P) or both, depending on the situation (A/P), and illustrates the feature by suggesting the position it would likely attract within the film industry.

Features in the Film Industry

Feature Characteristic	Example
1. Power	A
	Director- Producer
2. Vanity	A/P
	Actor- Critic- Art Director
3. Greed	A/P
	Producer- Financier- Advertisers
4. Self-Pity	P
	Gopher- Make-up Artist- Caterer-Understudy
5. Destructiveness	A
	Critic

6. Dominance	A Director- Producer
7. Fear	A/P Understudy; Person behind the scenes
8. Lunatic	A/P Special effects- Stuntman
9. Tramp	P Proofreaders- Assistants- Writers
10. Willfulness	P Editors-Legal staff
11. Naivete	A/P The audience
12. Nonexistence	P Composers- Hidden supporters

Any individual can play any part, on the stage or in life, and express any feature through any role. The examples above simply illuminate the particular craving each chief feature expresses – the stuntman's craving for the extremes of lunatic, the critic's penchant for destructiveness, and so on. Now we can explore each chief feature in greater detail.

POWER

Power is, in essence, a natural ability to intimidate. People with a chief feature of power will intimidate others whenever and wherever possible. Even if they have no "official" power, they will try to exercise whatever power they have, or to make a great show of having power.

People with a power feature are not concerned with what others think about them. There is no fear behind the exercise of power; rather, the individual gets a "charge" out of the exertion, believes he becomes more real, more alive, more identifiable as an individual.

We delight in reading about people with power features; that's why novels about power such as Master of the Game and Shogun, are sold in every airport. We love these books because we vicariously enjoy the exercise of power. Power is the most impatient of features.

A power feature is distinguishable from a fear feature, in that individuals with Fear can use power to hide fear. Power becomes a means to keep others from threatening them. Individuals with a Fear feature care about what others think, whereas individuals with power are generally insensitive or dismissive of public opinion. Power with concern may indicate a chief feature of Fear.

Power cannot be bothered with explanations; in the maintenance of power, no explanation is required, only more power. And while individuals with a Power feature are generally unconcerned with the impression they make on others, it is important for them not to be perceived as weak. They will do almost anything to appear strong, because weakness represents an absence of power. Thus, if an individual with a Power feature actually succumbs to an injury – for instance, they are physically hurt or ill – that person will try to override their injury, to make it appear as though the injury has no effect on them, has not made them weak. You'll see these persons running multi-million dollar businesses from their hospital bed while recovering from a heart attack, or running the family business from the bedroom during a fever.

A positive side of power is that it is good at getting things done. Power accomplishes goals. A power feature also excites the use of power in others. That is, sometimes we may find ourselves imitating power when we are around a person with power.

And each body type expresses power differently. For example, a Solar type with the chief feature of power often does not realize the effect or impact of its power. A Martial uses power like a club, a Mercury will be more devious, a Jovial will force you to except his hospitality.

VANITY

Vanity is, in essence, a natural tendency to seek or attract attention. Unlike Fear, a person with vanity wants to be seen. The important point for Vanity is that everybody "know" no matter what it does. Vanity craves to be noticed, attended to, cared for and coddled. Vanity, once recognized can motivate one to look within, as can any other chief feature.

Donald Trump has a chief feature of Vanity. At first, Trump's chief feature looks like Greed; however, what he really wants is not money but attention. He has enough money but not enough attention. Vanity never has enough attention. He would prefer positive attention, when his business is succeeding, but he also enjoys the attention he receives even when his business is failing. Trump doesn't make efforts to keep these failures out of the news; he enjoys being in the news. For example, Trump's penchant for dating young girls – making an obvious show of it – is a way of keeping himself in the news. A person with greed would tend to be more discreet, because money can be made more easily in the dark. Thus, a person with greed is often more prosperous by staying unknown; he doesn't need the attention, he needs the money. Paul McCartney, Warren Beatty, and Joan Collins have vanity. Barbra Streisand has vanity and power.

Elizabeth Taylor is another example of chief feature of vanity. Vanity is never happy with itself, never satisfied with its self-image, its worth, the level of respect it receives. Vanity never gets enough praise because it's looking for praise outside itself. Ultimately, people with vanity remain disturbed and dissatisfied, because vanity rarely appreciates its own success.

Vanity often requires immediate recognition and approval after it does or says something. People with vanity (especially Mercurial types with vanity) feel insecure if they do not receive an immediate applause, immediate recognition and approval. Vanity also tends to impress itself, to elevate itself by pointing out the obvious faults or strengths of other people. Still, as with each chief feature, vanity is first represented as energy, a mass of potential likely to go in a certain direction. The energy of vanity tends to produce vain people but it does not have to produce vain people. The same energy can be used to contemplate, to help others, to observe oneself (again it's the intention behind the feature which most interests us). Vanity may be "good" or "bad" depending on the person and the situation. For example, vanity can increase self-esteem. People with a chief feature of vanity feel like they mean something in this often indifferent world. Vanity helps us cope. Dress, grooming, putting on a nice coat, these are characteristics of vanity, but these tendencies can be uplifting, say, to someone who is depressed. Vanity requires a fairly refined level of presentation as it relates to the person's body type and alchemy. Vanity helps to make beauty a priority in the world.

By taking a neutral, more objective stance toward our chief feature; by seeing the feature as the Knowledge sees it, we can reduce the moral rigidity of the features ("vanity is a deadly sin," for example) and see the world more as other people see it.

GREED

Greed is, in essence, a natural tendency to desire and to be continually dissatisfied with desire. Greed tends to be a monetary feature, on the instinctive side, although there can be emotional greed, moving greed and intellectual greed. Individuals with the chief feature of greed will sacrifice health, friendship, country, almost anything to satisfy greed.

As Ivan Boesky once put it, "Greed is good." A person

with a greed feature will never have a large enough house, enough money in the bank, a ritzy enough wardrobe. They will always demand "more." Satisfying desire, for greed, only increases desire.

Our competitive world has created a global mind set epitomizing the greed feature. For instance, industrial greed has created a kamikaze-like approach to the environment. Industrial pollution, such as the unrestrained depletion of Brazil's rain forests, and the destruction of indigenous cultures has resulted from the drive for "more and more." Greed lacks overview.

The short-sightedness in modern business typifies the greed feature: immediate profits matter more than long-term objectives. As President Reagan said, "Our grandchildren will be paying for our mistakes." And so they will.

Like power, the greed feature feels no concern for other people. We can see this in contrast to vanity, which derives its value from interaction with people. With greed, people only have value in terms of what they can give or have taken from them.

Greed has a weak sense of humor because humor is giving, and greed is a taking feature. Greed wishes the products of attention, yet resists exposure. In response to the negative aspects of greed, which are considerable, elements of positivity can prevail. Greed can foster innovation, creativity, technological advancement and, in an effort to be always ahead, can employ a certain level of efficiency that will eliminate waste.

Greed can be found anywhere; it is a common human weakness, but it is not a common chief feature.

Greed is not the same as gluttony, although the reaction we have to a glutton is the same reaction we have to somebody with a greed feature.

Queen Elizabeth II and Nancy Reagan both have a chief

feature of greed. People with a power or greed feature tend to produce a sense of discomfort or threat in those around them, while people with a non-existence feature pass by unnoticed. People with a vanity feature automatically make us feel inferior to them, which then necessitates that we prove we're not inferior.

To verify chief feature we need to observe how others effect us, to note the reaction we have before we think about it. There are general reactions to features and specific reactions of features to features. A person with fear, for example, might like the protection offered by dominance where a person with power will fight it, or a non-existent person will see power as a means of existing, and vanity will see power as abusing existence, or self-pity will marvel at vanity's self-praise, and tramp will abhor it.

SELF-PITY

Self-pity is, in essence, a natural tendency to feel too much concern for one's self. Self-pity is always saying, "Woe is me, I deserve better." Or as Rodney Dangerfield puts it, "I tell you, I don't get no respect." Self-pity is the whining feature, to which most of us are prone in moments of extreme hardships.

The stand-in provides a good example of self-pity. A stand in is never good enough to be the lead; he's always waiting in the wings. He won't get paid enough, won't ever get enough attention, enough opportunity, enough love and respect. Although a stand-in pities himself and hates himself, for his self-pity, in reality, he is unconsciously looking for a position that makes him say, "Woe is me." This is the feature that gave birth to the notion that "misery loves company". If it isn't in a situation where it can despair, this feature will create one.

Acknowledging and exploring the patterns of chief feature increases self knowledge and yields a greater sense of control over one's life. For example, if you see yourself sliding into self pity, you don't have to pity yourself all the more for doing so. You can know that a part of you enjoys the self-pity, needs the self-pity, needs to express this feature wherever possible. Seeing this tendency, you can then resist. "I don't need to express this feature right now," you can say; take authority over it; see it as a tendency, rather than an inevitable moral failure on your part. You can try a little vanity or power instead.

It is difficult to see self-pity in one's self, because self-pity is not a proud or demonstrative feature, not happy to see what it is. Because individuals with self-pity have a need to feel sorry for themselves, they often attract humiliating circumstances and they regularly feel "too" sorry for other people as a means of justifying how sorry they feel towards themselves. The positive side of self-pity is that it can be transformed into a sense of critical empathy; a bridge to nurturing compassion for others. This feature, in its positive application, can manifest an emotional plea for urging others to rise to the challenge.

DESTRUCTIVENESS

Destructiveness is, in essence, a natural tendency to challenge. Destructiveness will challenge anything: people, situations, concepts. Destructiveness is always tearing something down or apart.

A person with a chief feature of destructiveness will not wish to reason with people. He will prefer a direct confrontation because confrontation encourages the possibility of destruction. He may try to reason for a while, but feeling that reason has not succeeded, he will not remain passive. Destructive types are never satisfied leaving situations unresolved; they prefer destruction to inaction, violence to passivity. Thus destructiveness tends to be an active feature: it breaks everything to pieces. By way of contrast, power usually employs logic; whereas with destructiveness, satisfaction comes in destroying the subject of conflict: another person, an object, even one's self. The destructive type's method of concluding a conflict is to destroy it. Naturally, destructiveness often implicates the Martial type. The Germans are the best example.

Destructiveness is a challenge to harmony. It challenges order, quietude. It wants to be disruptive, break things down, create change. When things are stagnant, destructiveness throws in a bomb. People who have a chief feature of destructiveness destroy their marriages, their jobs, their personal possessions, people who work for them. It is easier for them to destroy than to maintain or fix it.

Clear cutting in forests, the creation of explosives, Holy Wars, acids, insecticides, strip-mining, are all products of the feature of Destructiveness. A terrorist may have a chief feature of destructiveness, since terrorism relies on destruction; yet terrorism is, more often than not, a manifestation of the feature of lunatic. Destructive types want to eliminate things absolutely. If they kill a spider, they destroy it completely, smash it into an unrecognizable blur. There is little ulterior motive beyond that of destruction. A person with destructiveness will find logic of limited applicability. They will not want to deal with the situation anymore, but will resolve it with a bang.

Destructiveness is decisive, thinks in terms of total annihilation, as in genocide. Destructiveness can be deadly when combined with absolute power (for example, Hitler or Saddam Hussein, or a lunatic feature, say, Gaddafi).

Destructiveness can manifest in the intellectual center, as well as in the instinctive, moving and emotional centers. An intellectually centered type with a chief feature of destructiveness will do his best to destroy your beliefs; he will question your faith ad nauseam, and if he fails to destroy the belief, he will destroy you. Modern art, which subverts classical notions of beauty, line and rhythm, can be viewed as an expression of destructiveness in the intellectual and moving centers.

Like all features, destructiveness isn't in itself a bad feature. Indeed, spiritual work is inherently destructive: the old self must die before the new self can be born ("born again"); one must "die" into "life." And there are the examples of destroying old buildings to construct new ones, destroying lies, weaknesses, and evils. Each feature, Body type, Alchemy, and Center of focus are like a car, a weapon or a recipe. How we as individuals drive the car, use the weapon, serve the recipe, is the measure of a feature's positive or negative status. A means of evaluating Chief Features influence on "Character." Once again we seek to evaluate intent.

DOMINANCE

Dominance is, in essence, a natural ability- to subjugate others by persuasion and force of reason. What is correct for dominance, what feeds dominance, is correct for everyone, according to dominance. Dominance, instructs, teaches, lectures and preaches. Dominance thinks that to think other than how it thinks, is not thinking; that to do other than as dominance has said to do, is not doing. Next to dominance all other features are blind, according to dominance.

Dominance will attempt to convince its victims, its opponents, its children; to reassure them, but not destroy them, not waste their utility. Dominance wants everything from a person but not the individual in him. America, as a nation, has the chief feature of dominance and power. This is in harmony with its type, the Saturn-Mars type. Saturn is typically persuasive, while Mars is forceful. Thus, the United States has been both an economic and military superpower, dominating the world culturally and also controlling regions through military might.

Dominance aims to control by being more correct, more logical, more grandiose than others. Dominance is never content with "small potatoes," but must have great things. It must leave behind great works, great words, great buildings, great monuments, great forms of thought. For example, the English have dominance as a chief feature. They are always leaving rules behind them wherever they go.

Dominance tries either to be responsible or not to be responsible. It won't take the middle ground. If it can't be responsible, it will completely move away from something which is a kind of dominance by inversion or inaction. In sense they are dominating by employing the "take away theory" in refusing to be available, condone or participate.

Dominance seeks to find a way to make others dependent on it, to create an environment of dependence. This is why it is difficult to notice that one is being dominated. You do not become suddenly dependent on another person; you become dependent gradually.

The positive side of dominance is its flair for organization. And dominance can make people more civil as civility is needed to sustain dominance. Dominance is also good as an arbitrator, as people with dominance generally listen well.

FEAR

Fear is, in essence, a natural tendency to mistrust situations and people. Fear appears unreasonable to the other features, over-protective, overly defensive. One who has a chief feature of fear sees in every situation the possibility of something going awry, which will lead to danger and injury. A bread knife sitting carelessly on a table is a weapon, an open door, an invitation to rape or robbery.

Fear is a state of being overly concerned with possible disaster. People with a fear feature have more nightmares. They worry more, they seek out good luck charms and are more likely to believe in evil and the jinx. They are more suspicious of the invisible side of truth and life itself. They fear death, the fear life. No place is safe; there is no haven, no hiding place. People with fear are anxious people ever prepared for the sky to fall.

Where power has a decision making tendency and can act, fear paralyzes. People who have fear can panic, inside, and they disguise this panic in the feature of power hiding their fear through aggression. From the outside, they appear dynamic, forthright, forceful. But they are actually scared to death.

On the positive side, fear keeps us from walking down a dark alley, from eating bad food, from placing ourselves in situations of unreasonable danger. Fear in its proper perspective can be used to maintain high degrees of focus for extended periods of time when it is absolutely clear what must be done to survive.

LUNATIC

Lunatic is, in essence, a natural tendency to be extreme. Extreme anger, extreme joy, extreme piety, extreme depravity, extreme thinking, extreme mannerisms, extreme talk, extreme desires, for the feature of Lunatic extremes are normal. Lunatics are spontaneous, erratic, and unpredictable; they resist the dictates of authority. It is these tendencies that make us think of people with a lunacy feature as being "crazy," but they are not crazy, just extreme. And people with Lunatic often fail to understand how those around them can be so regular, boring, and uncreative.

A lunatic might become excessively distraught over losing a button, stubbing a toe, or forgetting a thought. It's difficult to become familiar with lunatics, to "know" them, as they very often change who we think they are. They like to keep the rest of the world guessing. Lunatics engage in an unreasonable waste of energy, in inappropriate responses, in brinkmanship.

Again, as with any feature, Lunatic in itself is neither good nor bad until after the establishment of intent. Moreover, once you begin to observe your chief feature, you can use this Knowledge to manifest a difference in behavior, if you choose to do so. For example, if you know your chief feature is Lunatic, that you bend towards extremes, when you find your behavior growing violent or outrageous, you can say to yourself, "Aha, there's that lunatic tendency again. I don't have to go along." You control the tendency; it does not control you. Intent then is based on "conscious" choice.

Howard Hughes had a lunatic feature. His behavior patterns were erratic and extreme. In his imagination, germs were larger than elephants. Though Howard Hughes was an unusual case, we all have lunatic moments.

In the midst of lunacy, you don't care what anybody thinks, logic cannot be applied. You don't care about normal standards. When this behavior becomes normal for you, that's lunatic. When someone says, "How are you," and you say, "I feel really really good," that's lunatic. Lunatics overdo everything from warmth to paranoia.

Lunatics with a gold alchemy will tend to be fanatical about refinement. They will be crazy about having every little thing in place, and this will make them aggravating to people around them. This is just one example of the way in which one tendency – here, chief feature – can interact with another tendency, such as alchemy. Destructive types with a gold alchemy, for example, will be planning the perfect revenge, every detail in place; whereas destructive types with a lead alchemy will just blow something up, start a fire, sink the whole ship.

As noted, lunatic seems crazy, but is really just a normal person conducting himself in an extreme manner. And it's difficult to reason with a lunatic type. If we confront someone with a lunatic feature, and try to express our point-of-view, they'll argue without reserve or completely shut off. A lunatic has no ears. It's much easier to persuade other features to act differently. Lunatic can't be persuaded with logic, reason or emotional appeal. Little else can direct a lunatic to change, or to contain itself – except physical force. On the positive side lunatic can create a demand for questioning and a re-evaluation of conventional logic. Though logic helps to balance society it can also act to atrophy social evolution. Lunatic can expose that atrophy.

TRAMP

Tramp is, in essence, a self-deprecating conviction that life exists without a hierarchy of value. A person with a tramp feature feels that all forms of self-discipline are a pointless infringement upon individual rights and freedoms, that moral standards are not worth supporting because they can only fail. But this sense of over-impending failure does not make the tramp sad or remorseful. On the contrary, tramp thrives on depravity and failure. Tramp lacks a value base and borrows values from other people.

People with a tramp feature often disregard authority, but in a passive manner. Unlike willfulness, which tends to resist authority, tramp often ignores or sidesteps authority. Tramp people justify that it is better not to do what they're told because, just because. Tramps have difficulty with responsibility; they are often attracted to drugs and unrestricted sexual adventures. They are a permissive lot who don't see the loss in losing self esteem, integrity, dignity or moral goodness.

Tramp overvalues or undervalues because it doesn't know what to value. The chief feature of our age is Tramp moving toward Lunatic. People with a tramp feature are unreliable, often failing to keep appointments or show up and are more frequently not good for their word.

Tramp sees no value in the lessons of history, the value of maintaining professional and moral standards. "Something for

131

nothing" is the tramp feature's motto. "Free" is the tramp features god, the most important word in its language. Tramp seeks the 'highs" of life without commitment. Much of modern and abstract art is tramp art; portraying nothing to mean something, or something to mean nothing.

And tramp feels it is owed something. It doesn't have to do anything to feel owed; simply by being alive, it feels that things must be given to it. Laziness and slothfulness are not in themselves indications of tramp, yet a tramp feature often is attracted to laziness and slothfulness. Tramps and Venusians may be difficult to distinguish, because both tend to an indifferent, blase, feel good, "it doesn't matter to me" attitude. But the distinguishing mark of tramp is its tendency to undervalue itself. The positive side of tramp is that, as a passive feature, it can embrace other perspectives and viewpoints, and does not puff itself up, turn away or manipulate. Tramp is the most flexible of features.

WILLFULNESS

Willfulness is in essence, a natural tendency to resist. Thus, willfulness is decisive yet stubborn like a mule, confrontational, yet in a passive way. Someone with willfulness will let you know where they stand, without moving. They will make it clear they are not going to budge, they will not change their mind.

Lunars are the type most subject to willfulness. People with willfulness neither wish to control nor to be controlled; they are neither followers nor leaders. They are singular – persons preferring their own world to that of anyone else.

People with willfulness often enjoy isolation or what others might call lonely spaces or places. Willfulness is not a sociable feature; self-containment is more important than group communication. Willfulness does things to make other people aggressive toward it; then it can resist. In this sense willfulness can be active.

The positive side of willfulness is in its tendency not to give up. For instance, sometimes it is appropriate to say, "we shall not be moved." Willfulness forced desegregation in America, as well as many other beneficial changes in the legal and social structure of the country. Similarly, Gandhi's strategy of non-violence, though seemingly passive, actually embodied willfulness, which had the effect of forcing change upon a recalcitrant regime.

NAIVETE

Naivete is, in essence, a natural tendency to manifest or assume innocence. An individual with naivete will try to avoid assuming responsibility for others because he knows intuitively that he does not have the ability to control other people. Within he feels that other people are sharper; others have all the answers; he alone doesn't know enough. Therefore, he does not want to be put in a position where others are made dependent upon him.

You will find someone with a chief feature of naivete working in important yet non-responsible jobs like the arts, secondary or background character work, fashion design, as assistants, helpers, runners, illustrators, tour guides, kindergarten teachers, etc.

Marilyn Monroe exemplifies naivete, a feature that became the tragedy of her life. Children have naivete. There is something about them that puts you at ease. You know they are not looking at your faults. They are simply there, wide-eyed. They are not calculating how to take advantage of you. The naivete feature makes a person less manipulative.

A person with naivete will have a high degree of childishness. They won't expect anyone to take advantage of them. They want to play. Children play, they don't work; they don't have to take responsibility for their actions. People with naivete trust everyone, believe what is said without searching for hidden meanings, without suspecting a lie. They think no harm will come to them no matter what they do. They are the kids that never grow up, never grow old. It's hard for those with naivete to either be serious or be taken seriously. They are not heavy, but light like sunlight shimmering on a butterfly's wings. The chief feature of the Solar Type is naivete.

Naivete is generally passive. It doesn't "bite" like an active feature. It's not confrontational. Naivete doesn't ordinarily cause problems; problems happen to a person with naivete.

NON-EXISTENCE

Non-existence, in essence, is a natural tendency to conceal, to dissolve one's identity into another person, thing, or nothing. A person with a chief feature of non-existence can conceal anything, but most of all he conceals himself. You'll find people subject to non-existence in the background, behind the scenes, as invisible as possible. People who would make the best spies are those with a chief feature of non-existence. We just don't notice people with this feature.

Non-existence is passive; it will yield its space because it has no sense of its own space. People who we remember yet whose names we forget may have non-existence. They don't make a strong enough impression. Non-existent types live through other people, get their identity through others identities. Non-existence is a failure to recognize obstacles, not freedom from them.

People around the office with non-existence are good workers. They don't question authority, they follow rules, they believe without doubt. People who are easy to please, who don't mind losing or being inconvenienced manifest non-existence. Our society – the so called masses – manifests non-existence, with its narcotic dependence on television, obedience to regulation, authority and fashion.

Non-existence can absorb a lot of negativity without realizing it. When non-existence realizes it has absorbed negativity, it retaliates, becomes negative in return, reflects in action the negativity it's absorbed; it copies the negativity like a copy machine, does not express it's own negativity but that of someone else.

Chief Feature and Role Playing

When directors are casting for a film, they are looking, to a certain extent, for particular features. For example, if you are trying to cast the role for a noncommittal, laid-back character, you might select Mickey Rourke. His tramp feature makes him ideal for roles where the character swims in depravity and failure. If, on the other hand, you're looking for a commanding figure, say, to play Queen Elizabeth I, Glenda Jackson is a natural choice, her power feature and Martial body type create the needed sense of command and authority. She walks, speaks, dresses, and generally presents herself with a definite purpose, a convincing and believable charge; whatever role she plays, she expresses power. If you need someone to go crazy, like the protagonist in the film, "Frances," you will choose someone like Jessica Lange, as she has a chief feature of lunatic which is erratic, spontaneous to a fault, not necessarily crazy, but completely unpredictable. A good casting agent would want this Knowledge. They would want to be on the cutting edge in being attuned to the actor's natural capacities from many vantage points. Many agents have some of this knowledge intuitively and seem to see the actor's chief feature, his type, alchemy and center of focus. A movie critic would benefit as well in pinpointing the pitfalls and highlights of a film. Often times it's the casting that didn't work. This could cost a substantial amount of money in the end regardless of whether it hits the financial marks of success. "Broken Arrow" was a good example of this. If the starring roles had been reversed, the box office revenues would have been even greater. The main evil character in this film is an explosive and destructive type and John Travolta, a Venusian-Mercury, a sympathetic yet devious type does not epitomize destructiveness where a Martial would. Christian Slater is a Martial and would have been more believable cast in the role of the antagonist. When Travolta speaks of destroying or blowing something up, we don't believe him. If he says he's going to destroy something you know he is also going to keep something for himself, he is not fully committed to the act of destruction. However, a Martial is fully committed and will invest everything into annihilating it and removing it from the face of the earth.

The roles individuals assume in life also reveal their chief feature. Indeed, in professional and personal relationships, people often look for a feature that will allow them to best express their own chief feature. For example, an individual with a fear feature will look for someone with a feature that protects them. Thus you'll find someone with a fear feature married to someone with dominance or power. The person with fear will actually enjoy being subservient, if such subservience provides protection. For example, Dennis Thatcher and Prince Phillip both have fear and nonexistence; both are comfortable protected by their more powerful wives. Likewise, an individual with vanity will be comfortable with tramp, because a vanity feature overvalues itself and tramp undervalues itself. Greed can do well with naivete, as naivete will make a game of the excesses of greed. Self-pity and nonexistence support each other. Destructiveness will attract more attention, which pleases lunatic, etc., etc.

Possible Origins of Chief Feature

Chief features can come from several places. Many religious traditions claim that we are born with weaknesses derived from a past life. There may be lessons left unlearned in their lives, or certain failures or successes, or even influences transmitted from people we knew in those lives.

Chief feature may also be acquired during childhood. For example, let us say that at age seven your father beat you. As a result, you become particularly sensitized to violence. You develop an inner attitude of fear. At first, the fear is specific, you are afraid of your father. As you grow older, the fear begins to generalize. It becomes fear of pain, and then fear of people and of your environment. Fear of men. Fear of women. Fear of driving too fast, fear of falling, fear of not saying the right thing at the right time, fear of not having enough money, fear of having too much money, fear of anything. Fear permeates your life. Once it is a chief feature, your personality revolves around fear, you become "fear of____." The fear engendered in childhood becomes a complete view of your life, of your relationship to the world. All your attitudes about relationships, about travel, about employment, and so on become filtered through the chief feature. You decide to be or not to be with someone because of the level of fear that they produce, to take or not to take a certain job because of fear rather than conscience or logic. Chief feature is an enormous weight on us. It creates pressure, subconsciously, causing one to make certain decisions that are not necessarily in their best interest.

When people are told about their chief feature, they feel uncomfortable. Chief feature is strong in us. We tend to deny its presence. Unconsciously, we think we need it and we depend on it. Chief feature is reliable – it is always there to excuse and justify our weaknesses. Like a dial tone – you pick up the phone and it's there. Any situation you are in, chief feature is the fault that appears strong because it is reliable.

In fact, chief feature eventually becomes indispensable to "personality" as a perceived requisite for our survival. People are afraid to face new situations without the chief feature. For example, if a person afraid of flying removed his fear he might actually enjoy flying – and thus contradict the view he had nourished and cherished for years with regards to flying's threat.

Ambivalent Aspects of Chief Feature

Chief feature is something we hide behind – something that hides behind us. Each chief feature has a positive side which can be expressed if the person observes and struggles against chief feature. Thus chief feature is essentially a bank account of energy. Typically, the energy is drawn out of the account in limited ways by circumstance-not by individual choice, not by intent decided upon by us. We don't know that the bank account exists. The "money" (energy) is withdrawn whenever an outside stimulus acts upon it.

Once you become aware of the account, you begin to have some control over it. In some situations, for example, power is what you need; in others, fear; in still others, destructiveness. If you are confronted with a mugger at gunpoint, it is foolish to manifest a power feature; fear or nonexistence may be more appropriate. Normally, we react; we do not act. Choice is not ours. With knowledge and an increased alertness we can learn to see ahead of chief feature, to formulate an action supportive of multiple perspectives, spiritual evolution and greater productivity. We will have more energy as the consumption of weaknesses vitalizes the soul; expands our senses beyond sense perception.

Features tend to replace one another. If a person's chief feature is fear, that person might respond to manifestations of fear with power. Vanity might respond with destructiveness, self-pity with nonexistence. One feature will often work on or for another. Progress is made by understanding all features, not just the one or two which are particular to us.

All features are dualistic and absolutist. Nonexistence sees itself as existing through others or not existing at all. Fear sees itself as being either safe or constantly in danger. Greed sees itself as either having everything or nothing. Power sees itself as either being controlled or controlling. Vanity will see itself as either being complimented or criticized. Tramp sees itself as either having great value or no value at all. Moreover, each chief feature has its own morality, its own view of what is important. Take, for example, your first day in a new job. Someone with power might say, "the most important thing is to amass power: on the job, in the family, in society." Someone with lunatic might say: "as long as I express my individuality, and don't get swallowed up by the corporation, I'm all right." Someone with fear might say:"As long as I survive, everything is okay." Tramp might say: "as long as the job's relaxed and I can take it easy." Nonexistence might say: "just stay invisible, in the background." Each one looks at its point-of view as "right"; another view is "wrong." But each one unto itself is right. And we can move among the features because each of us has access to each feature. We all have every body type, every alchemy, chief feature and center of focus within us. The only differences are in degree. Chief feature generates that attitude in us which believes more in the weaknesses in other people rather than their strengths. Generally we look at someone to find out where their faults are, how well can we compete with them. This is our chief feature. It takes a weakness to recognize a weakness.

The feature of the country in which an individual lives modifies the feature of the individual. For example, in a country like Germany, which has a chief feature of power, you will find many individuals with diverse chief features, who have a tendency to express power. In India, a country with a passive feature, that of nonexistence, you find many people with active features-such as dominance, power and greed who express those features in a less insidious and destructive way.

All features appear positive when they have their way. We could call this a crime high. We must watch ourselves, attempt to objectively determine if our pleasures come from a loss of integrity, if we are made happy at another's expense. If so, our happiness is not ours and it will one day turn on us.

Chief Feature and Awakening

As with each of the "tendencies" listed in this book, chief feature can be viewed as a seed planted in us which grows to varying degrees. Hitler had a power feature, but the economic and political circumstances surrounding him enabled that power feature to dominate the whole of his being. In most individuals chief feature does not consume the entire psyche. This permits us to escape, to gain control of the feature.

Like body type and alchemy, chief feature expresses itself through us. It is the feature that seeks expression, rather than we who choose to express the feature. At first it may seem strange to think of the Solar type, the gold alchemy, or the chief feature as external "entities" with minds and agendas all their own who express themselves through us. Yet, if we begin observing these "entities," we will see that they are, indeed, separate from us, and they are intelligent, that very often they know more about us than we know about ourselves. And they act independently of our awareness of ourselves. Features manifest in us whether we decide to allow them or not. Thus, we can say that chief feature cares only about itself or feature gratification not about how "we" (our overall being) is affected by such gratification.

(Consider how much anger thinks of our welfare when it lashes out against someone we love.) Chief feature siphons off of the energy of compassion and healing. Chief feature is opinionated, overly competitive, selfish and extremely cunning. Yet, by acknowledging the presence of chief feature, we can begin to weaken its hold on our lives, to transform weakness into strength.

Let's take the chief feature of power for example. It wants to be in a position of power. To feed on power. It needs to acquire or produce situations which allows it to express itself, to satisfy its appetite. Perhaps you have a chief feature of power and you're working in an office. It's not fair or moral for you to cut someone out of a job, or maybe even as a practical matter you would be best served by working with him. But your chief feature doesn't care. Cutting someone out is an expression of power. It "feels" good, makes the acquisition of power more real and more necessary. Because your overall aim is to run the office you don't wait until the title "king of the office" is bestowed upon you before you exercise power, you push all the way. Rather than working with that someone, or appreciating him, or helping him, you devise a way to eliminate him, make him so subservient to you that he is powerless in the office and can only do what you say.

At the time you are moving toward fulfillment of chief feature's hunger, everything else in your life, or in that particular situation is moving toward it as well, even though "you" – the whole person – may have different goals. Thus, the chief feature accounts for many of our worst arguments. Chief feature is the psychological wall that makes us rigid, lacks flexibility, diversity and spiritual understanding. It's the architect of our misconception of moral right and moral justice; chief feature tends to turn toward the negative, and once set in motion, is difficult to stop. All chief features make us insatiably possessive of both our weaknesses and our strengths. By that possession, our perspective is reduced to a one-dimensional and sub-jective evaluation of life. We see "I" as uniquely singular and profoundly important; we lack an evolving multi-dimensional perspective. To be possessed by chief feature is to remain as a marionette, stranded on the tentacle threads of some desper-ate puppeteer.

Tendency Chart #9 – Chief Feature

Chief Feature	Active/Positive Feature Tendency	Positive Attributes	Negative Attributes
POWER	A	ACCOMPLISHMENT	INTIMIDATION
VANITY	A OR P	AESTHETIC SENSIBILITY	SELF INDULGENT
GREED	P OR A	MONETARY DISCERNMENT	EXCESSIVE CONSUMPTION
SELF-PITY	P	COMPASSION	CHRONIC WHINING
DESTRUCTIVENESS	A	INITIATES CHANGE	GRATUITOUS VIOLENCE
DOMINANCE	A	CREATES ORDER	MANIPULATIVE PERSUASION
FEAR	A OR P	CIRCUMSPECTION	PARANOIA
LUNATIC	A	SPONTANEITY	FANATICISM
TRAMP	P	NON-ATTACHMENT	SELF-DEPRAVATION
WILLFULNESS	P	PERSEVERANCE	STUBBORNNESS
NAIVETE	P OR A	OPTIMISTIC	IMMATURITY
NON-EXISTENCE	P	HUMILITY	UNAVAILABILITY

Tendency Chart #10 – Chief Feature

Feature	Person	Place	Other Examples
POWER	MARGARET THATCHER JFK GENERAL PATTON GLENDA JACKSON	SOUTH AFRICA MUNICH	SHARK PIT BULL DIRECTOR PRODUCER CEO
VANITY	ELIZABETH TAYLOR KEVIN COSTNER TRUMP	FRANCE PARIS	PEACOCK ACTOR MODEL DESIGNER
GREED	IVAN BOESKY MICHAEL MILKEN NANCY REAGAN QUEEN ELIZABETH II FERDINAND MARCOS	KUWAIT WALL STREET	COYOTE JACKEL PRODUCER FINANCIER PHYSICIAN
SELF-PITY	PATTY DAVIS BETTE MIDLER	LEPER'S COLONY HOSPITALS	BLOODHOUND PATIENT
DESTRUCTIVENESS	GODZILLA MEL GIBSON CHUCK NORRIS MIKE TYSON	GERMANY IRAQ	MAFIA TYPHOON RUGBY CRITIC CORONER
DOMINANCE	CHARLETON HESTON RONALD REAGAN JULIE ANDREWS ABRAHAM LINCOLN	ENGLAND LONDON WASHINGTON DC	STATUE OF LIBERTY EIFLE TOWER WORLD TRADE CENTER MT. EVEREST NURSING ADMIN.
FEAR	RINGO STARR JUDY GARLAND	NORTH KOREA HONG KONG HAITI	EELS GROUNDHOG MINORITIES PATIENT UNDERSTUDY
LUNATIC	QUADDAFI IDI AMIN NICHOLAS CAGE	IRAN LIBYA	MATING SEASONS TERRORISTS KAMAKAZIS PSYCHIATRIC STAFF STUNTMAN

Continued...

Feature	Person	Place	Other Examples
TRAMP	MICKEY ROURKE JACK NICHOLSON DENNIS HOPPER	MEXICO	VAGABONDS HOMELESS BUMS SCREENWRITERS
WILLFULNESS	SHAMIR GEORGE BUSH	SWITZERLAND	MULES EDITORS LEGISLATORS REGULATORS
NAIVETE	MARILYN MONROE	SWEDEN	DOLPHINS BUTTERFLIES CANDY STRIPERS AUDIENCE
NON-EXISTENCE	DENNIS THATCHER PRINCE PHILLIP	MONGOLIA CANADA	SHADOWS MOLES SET DESIGNERS

Tendency Chart #11 – Chief Feature

Likely progression following saturation of the primary or chief feature

Saturations of **Chief Feature**	Moves towards **Secondary Feature**	Followed by movement towards **Tertiary Feature**
POWER	DESTRUCTIVENESS	GREED
VANITY	NON-EXISTENCE	TRAMP
GREED	SELF-PITY	LUNATIC
SELF-PITY	FEAR	WILLFULNESS
DESTRUCTIVENESS	POWER	DOMINANCE
DOMINANCE	NON-EXISTENCE	POWER
FEAR	POWER	LUNATIC
LUNATIC	POWER	FEAR
TRAMP	LUNATIC	GREED
WILLFULNESS	POWER	DESTRUCTIVENESS
NAIVETE	FEAR	SELF-PITY
NON-EXISTENCE	TRAMP	WILLFULNESS

The Four Brains
or
Centers of Focus

Center of Focus and Attention

All human beings have within them not one, but several different "brains" or "centers" of intelligence which determine orientation and response to the world around and within them. Each center represents a different form or quality of intelligence, a different approach to understanding and digesting or processing experience. There are four such centers; intellectual, emotional, instinctive, and moving. The intellectual center finds its reality in thoughts and words, rather than emotions, movements or sensations. The emotional center prefers emotions, feelings and the multiple revelations of perceptual vision. The moving center focuses on gestures, sport, the comforting joy of performing repetitious duties. The instinctive center revels in the sensory experience of food, sex, drugs, massage, tub baths, pampering vacations.

The primary significance of this four-part categorization is that it dispels the myth of the singular and unified personality, and allows for a more fluid understanding of human interaction. We truly are a multi-dimensional composite of four very different orders of intelligence. Each center, or brain, sees one aspect of the world as being more real, satisfying and more justified in its right to exist. Thus, an intellectually-centered person (someone with a center of focus in the intellectual center) will approach most situations predominately from an intellectual point-of-view, an emotionally-centered person will take the emotional perspective, a moving-centered person will focus on movement and spatial relations and an instinctively-centered person on sensation.

These divergent orientations will account for conflicts and misunderstandings based on different unconscious preferences and predispositions. Take, for example, the Jones family, which can never seem to agree on anything. They enter a video store in search of an evening's entertainment. Irma, the intellectually-centered mother, selects a documentary on World War II – or maybe an Ingmar Bergman film. Sam, the emotionally-centered father, condemns his wife's "brainy taste" and calls her an "egghead." He'd rather watch an old classic, maybe "Casablanca," or even "Love Story" – but the sappy sentimentals, for an intellectually-centered type are repulsive. Their son, Morris, the moving-centered type, has selected James Bond, with races, chases, and no one sitting still. His sister, Ida, the instinctively-centered type, has picked up a video which studies the relationship between food and sex.

The family squabbles, they can't agree on a movie, and each ends up doing his own thing. Irma stays home reading Paul Johnson's "A History of the Jews." Sam reviews old photographs of his family, or maybe tinkers with his stamp collection. Morris, a Saturn-Mars type, has wrestled control of the VCR. He's watching James Bond. Ida is at her boyfriend's house pouring chocolate sauce all over his body.

The next day they're at the bookstore, trying to pick out a present for Grandma. Irma is in the mystery section, checking out the Sherlock Holmes series; Sam is reviewing trashy best-sellers; Morris is wagging his finger at a sales clerk in confrontation over a price tag; Ida is in the food section.

We can use almost any activity, any subject, and see center of focus at work. Suppose you are in the store trying to find a greeting card for your brother who is about to get married, or your friend, who is in the hospital, or your colleague, who has just gotten a promotion. What kind of card will attract your attention?

An intellectually-centered person will want a card that is well-written, one that satisfies the intellect. He'll want something clever and witty – maybe something with a Doonesbury cartoon. The Hallmark slogan – "when you care enough to send the very best" – will make him nauseous. He's caring, but the word "care" has an emotional resonance that the intellectual center will not feel. An emotionally-centered person will select a card that is highly symbolic, since the emotions deal more with symbols than with numbers and letters and mental formulae. A moving-centered person will buy a pop-up card, or maybe one that's folded over several times, or one that shows figures in motion. An instinctively-centered person will want something sensual. Maybe a card talking about sex, or being overweight, or just wanting to touch – "you know I miss the sensation of your body beside me." The card will be related to sensation and how sensation defines reality. In each case the individual selects the "right" greeting card based on his own center of focus – but what about considering the center of focus of the recipient? Spouses, lovers, employees, bosses and friends can get the wrong message if you send a signal based on your center of focus.

Identifying Center of Focus

To verify which center of focus dominates in us, we need to observe what we reach for first; thoughts, emotions, movement or sensation.

We can also examine typical activities and reactions. What do I like to do in my leisure hours? Read a book, watch a soap opera, play golf or take a long hot bath? How do I tend to react to conflict? When someone makes me angry, do I respond with some theoretical justification for my behavior (intellectual response), do I shout or scream or cry (emotional response), do I throw things (moving response), or do I feel pain in my body, a threat to my physical well being (instinctive response).

When I watch the evening news, do I respond with a theory about international foreign policy, or with anger or affinity toward some politician, or do I turn away and wash dishes or eat a dessert? If a stimulus is too intellectual, do I shut down or ignore it? If it is too emotional, do I go into my theories and abstractions? If it involves too much activity, do I turn it off? If it is too sensual, do I find myself laughing or disgusted?

The four brains can be observed at a funeral or wedding. For example, one person is thinking about the meaning of death or marriage rites; another is crying his eyes out; a third is pacing around the church or synagogue; a fourth is embracing and touching other people.

Determining which is our center of focus can help us in relationships and professional objectives. Knowing our perceptual bias permits us an escape from subjective intolerance and misunderstanding and allows us to see what is "real" for other people. We become less critical, seeing our own likes and dislikes as preferences and tendencies built into our critical faculty via center of focus.

INTELLECTUAL

Intellectually-centered people can appear slow, or uncoordinated because their first automatic response is to think about things, whereas a moving-centered person's automatic reaction is to move. Intellectually-centered individuals tend to make everything they say sound factual or academic. The "Nerd" image tends to epitomize intellectual types. Intellectual types find the display of emotions repulsive and uncivilized.

You find intellectually-centered people in law firms. A lot

of sciences attract intellectually-centered people. Also, the intellectual parts of each center, such as the intellectual part of the moving center, the intellectual part of the emotional center, and the intellectual part of the instinctive center, will be involved in science, mathematics, psychological calculations, research, etc. The Internal Revenue Service is an intellectually-centered organization, and tax accountants are often intellectually-centered. Intellectual types tend to lack spontaneity, they "think" too much. They are too formal, rely too much on definitions. Names for them are more real than the person or thing being named. The market value of name recognition is an example of the intellectual center influencing societal behavior. People now buy the names of artists, the names of cars, the names of countries. A watch named Rolex sells better than exactly the same watch named Simon.

EMOTIONAL

Many emotional types tend to shy away from the gregarious emotional expression of, say, a Jovial type. Most tend to express subtle emotions, preferring an intimate exchange of feelings and concerns. The emotional brain tends toward the symbolic and archetypal, the sensitive or perceptual world

Emotionally-centered types will want to be seen as being emotionally sympathetic, emotionally warm, emotionally caring, emotionally alert, emotionally educated. They are going to pick a card, a gift, a vacation spot, a friend that reflects the emotional center of focus.

Emotionally-centered people live in a world of dynamic relations, of high emotional drama, just as intellectually-centered types live in a labyrinth of thoughts, moving types in excessive activity, instinctive types in frequent need of sensual stimulation. Emotionally-centered people have to be in environments where they can exchange feelings. Not many will take night jobs, for example, that require solo work. They will be attracted to professions such as medicine, health fields, singing, social work, psychiatry, psychology. Emotionally-centered types are subject to weight fluctuation even to the extreme when they are disturbed, hurt or angry. They are often plump, soft-bodied people whose haven for losing weight resides in perusing a further development of the other, more inactive, brains and parts of centers.

INSTINCTIVE

Instinctively-centered people are often healthy-looking and health conscious. They tend to recover quickly when ill or don't get ill as often as other types. They tend to be sensual, stocky and strong with thick hands and necks, legs, etc. They have more acute hearing and greater awareness of potential danger. They appear best equipped to survive on this planet, like elephants and rhinos. Body builders are often instinctively-centered, because building the body requires a consistent interest in the body.

The instinctive center in each of us often tries to make the other centers in us or another person appear responsible for its mistakes. For example, let's say you burped publicly. You might laugh in a way that makes the emotional center appear responsible, as though you intended the burps to be a joke, that there was foolish humor in the action, that you did not actually lose control.

And there is a dark side to the instinctive center represented in all humans by such evil figures as Wicked Witches and Satan. This, the powerful negative half of the intellectual part of instinctive center is secretive, cunning and ruthless. Witchcraft images and rituals of evil and violence, psychological darkness and black magic all reveal aspects of the negative half of the intellectual part of instinctive center, the extreme to which some people and even nations are drawn.

MOVING

Moving-centered individuals are always doing something related to movement; going somewhere, coming to see you, changing activities, or just pacing at the door. They are the most restless of the four centers of gravity, the least capable of sitting down, the least satisfied with the routine of one job.

Moving-centered people rely on movement, animated description and facial gesture to convey humor; whereas emotionally-centered people rely on emotions, will try to make people feel their humor, and intellectually-centered people work to make the audience think something is funny. Charlie Chaplin was a moving-centered type who pioneered the humor of slapstick movements. Most humor in silent movies is moving-centered. Comics understand this, and use the moving-center to convey their humor, emphasizing facial expressions and body gestures as much as text to tell jokes.

Prince Charles is a typical moving-centered type (the instinctive part). He is constantly in motion, fidgeting, adjusting his cuffs, posture, painting, playing polo, globetrotting, something.

Activities that relate to "doing something," such as dancing or walking (emotional types "take a stroll"), stimulate and feed the moving-center. Choreography, interior design, sports, dance, graphics, construction, driving, running errands, and flying are jobs that appeal to the moving-centered types.

Most athletes, dancers and sportsmen are moving-centered people. Moving types must move. They along with the Mercurials and Martials are the people who can't sit still in church, at graduation, in the board room: the ones in the family photo who moved just as the shutter clicked.

Moving types are visual types, spatially alert, coordinated, good with their hands, quick learners when it comes to sports. Each center of focus is quick to learn in areas related to its strengths. And memories within the four centers are easiest to

retrieve from that center which is our center of focus
Intellectually-centered types remember what was said, emo
tional types what was felt, moving types what was done
instinctive types what they sensed.

PARTS OF CENTERS

Each center has four parts: intellectual, emotional, moving
and instinctive. The common deck of playing cards, created
by the ancients to represent or chart human behavior
demonstrates the relationships between centers and parts o
centers. *See Chart on page 172.*

Each center is designated by one suit. The intellectua
center is represented by diamonds; the emotional center by
hearts; the moving center by the spades; and the instinctive
center by the clubs. The intellectual parts of each center are
represented by the Kings; the emotional parts by the Queens
and, for simplicity's sake, the moving and the instinctive
parts are combined and are called the "moving-instinctive"
parts, which are represented by the Jacks. Thus, we can look
across the centers to the parts and speak of the "kings" (the
intellectual parts the centers), the "queens" (the emotiona
parts of the centers), and the "jacks" (the moving-instinctive parts of the centers).

Most of the global population, perhaps 60%, is centered ir
the Jacks. There are fewer people in the Queens of centers and
even fewer in the Kings.

Original or creative thoughts and actions do not begin ir
the Jacks. The Jacks are the store houses of the average in us
the keepers of habit. When we are imitative, predictable
repetitive, we are in the Jacks.

Each of the Kings, Queens, and Jacks has four, or in our sim-
plified model, three, parts: intellectual, emotional, moving
instinctive. These are represented respectively by the tens

sevens, and fours; the nines, sixes and threes; and the eights, fives, and twos. It would take a whole book to describe in detail the kinds of activities and responses typically expressive of each part of a part of a center. We will highlight, therefore, only some of the parts of parts remembering that no part is "good" or "bad" in and of itself; each has its negative manifestations and its bright side.

JACK OF HEARTS: The instinctive or moving part of the emotional center is represented here. The Jack of Hearts is the manufacturer of "crowd emotions" or "group emotions." Mass marketing attempts to manipulate, stimulate and program the lifestyle values the Jack of Hearts. Smart advertisers are adept at harvesting the collective feelings evident in patriotism, fashion, sports, religion, etc. They cannot sell their products without first selling a lifestyle which will consume their products. Without knowing why, market strategists do know that the Jack of Hearts, once it starts to buy, will keep on buying. Emotional repetition is a function of the Jack of Hearts.

KING OF DIAMONDS (Intellectual Part of the Intellectual Center): Edison, Einstein and Newton were King of Diamond types. We have very little understanding of what motivates King of Diamonds people. They are curious, not unfriendly exactly but they have almost no need to understand emotional relationships. If they're lucky they'll find a spouse who will tolerate, accept and love them without demanding to be understood nor to understand. The King of Diamonds in a sense represents pure thought: the process of thinking for the sake of thinking.

SEVEN OF DIAMONDS: This card embodies the intellectual part of the emotional part of the intellectual center, which means that an individual with this part as his center

of gravity will first be intellectual, secondly emotional
and thirdly intellectual. Having two intellectual part
and one emotional part the Seven of Diamonds is intel
lectual in the extreme, like the King of Diamonds type
but not intensely aloof.

The Queen of Diamonds enjoys the excitement of learning
The King of Diamonds is more a learning work-horse, which
looks for factual verification, theoretical completeness and so
on. The Queen represents a love of learning, the seven, si:
and five, all of which are subsumed under the Queen, expres
a different approach to the love of learning. The six, the emo
tional part, is someone who likes reading books just for the
pleasure of reading and taking in information; they don't plar
to do anything with the information. The seven will have ar
intellectual purpose behind the reading, a master plan. The
five, the moving or instinctive part, will apply its intellect and
emotions to accomplish a moving or instinctive purpose.

KING OF CLUBS: This card represents survival intelli
gence, the intelligence that runs our bodies, that paces citie
full of intersecting pedestrians; the mind that prevents thou
sands of people from converging on a particular subwa·
entrance at the same time. The King of Clubs in its uniquel·
secretive fashion, is always organizing things. If too many peo
ple converge on one spot simultaneously, they'll crush eacl
other and die. This is not something we focus on consciousl)
but the King of Clubs is always there, alert at every intersec
tion of our life trying to keep us from killing ourselves or bein;
killed. Accidental death, especially among the young, is ofter
the result of a weak King of Clubs. The King of Clubs usuall·
calculates well enough into the future to insure that the indi
vidual survives. And like most Kings, its wants dictatoria
control over all the centers.

Psychic capacities, premonitions and ESP are instinctive

center capacities. The King of Clubs is intensely perceptive about the nature of the human organism. Its functions appear psychic because most people are not centered in the King of Clubs. But what the King does is not supernatural. People centered in the King of Clubs have a greater capacity to anticipate behavior, to foresee future events, to heal and manipulate the body. This can appear as mind-reading, miraculous, or even devious.

When a King of Clubs type walks into a room, it is understood immediately that he be taken seriously no matter what he says or does. Instinctively-centered people walking down the street do not strike the casual observer as defenseless. They seem strong, sure of themselves, they know something about us that nobody else knows; we fear that in them.

Religions propagated by the negative half of the King of Clubs often exploit followers with the fear of physical pain or punishment. The positive side of the King of Clubs will reward followers with physical pleasure, such as massage, sex, eating, and so on. This was the Rajneesh view of spirituality. The cannibal, teachers and followers who extol the virtues of human sacrifice, serial killers; all are examples of what happens when the negative half of the King of Clubs connects to chief feature. And in many cases to that of the chief feature of Lunatic. When the negative half of the King of Clubs combines with chief feature we come to the home of the devil in man; the domain where night conceals night and darkness spreads as an endless pleasure in creating pain. The King of Clubs controls the senses, thus it controls the whole of our physical person. The negative half of the King of Clubs is that side of our human being capable of eating another human being. All concepts of evil have their roots here. Whereas concepts of God come from the positive half of the intellectual part of the emotional center (The King of Hearts).

KINGS: Many scientists are centered in the intellectual parts of their centers. Physicist Henry Stapp in California, Rupert Sheldrake and Stephen Hawkins in England, for example, all represent the Kings. The Kings decipher abstractions; envision theories, formulas, whole processes, concepts; out of nothing, they harvest new ideas.

The Kings differ, however, in each of the four suits. We can see subtle distinctions between several of these "cards" if we compare our three scientists Rupert Sheldrake, Henry Stapp and Stephen Hawkins. Sheldrake is in the emotional part of the intellectual part of the emotional center. (The Nine of Hearts.) His theory of morphogenic resonance, though well documented, requires an awakening of emotional perception in the reader to understand its importance.

Stapp is in the instinctive part of the intellectual part of the intellectual center (The Eight of Diamonds.) His approach to physics is austere and factual and follows an orderly set of logical gains made by people ahead of him. And Hawkins is in the intellectual part of the intellectual part of the moving center (the Ten of Spades). Hawkins visualizes the universe as a moving mass of perfectly interactive forces, guided by the relationships of various mathematical formulas. The emphasis on wholistic systems, complete processes, balance, totality and harmony illustrates the basic nature of all the parts of all the Kings of centers. And there is an admission, or an awareness in each King of the value and necessity of employing emotional perception as a tool to measure and calculate the mysteries of life. In Western society, we tend to regard logic and the intellectual as a test of reality. We are only beginning to give the other centers their due, acknowledging the validity of ritual and myth as sources of truth beyond the dogmas of the scientific realm.

QUEENS: The Queens of centers represent our greates

need for other people, for spontaneity, excitement and drama. For the Queens, situations and places are meaningless without people. Beauty, wealth, grand vistas of nature and antiquity – without people, they are dead. Home life, clubs, birthday parties, gossip, intense intimacy, gambling, emotional adventure – these are the Queens special interests.

JACKS: The Jacks of centers are where we perform repetitious duties, repeat our daily 'good mornings' and 'good nights'; our daily likes and dislikes. The Jacks, like well behaved file cabinets, store memory, are generally easy to satisfy, are predictable and reliable. Habits are in the Jacks. After we have learned how to do something the Jacks take over. They put what we have learned into practice, transform feelings and ideas into daily routines.

The Jack of Spades (represented by the four, three and two of Spades), drives our cars, rides our bikes, runs, walks, swims, skates, flies. Anything that requires sustained movement is in the Jack. The Jack of the moving center runs on momentum: once it starts running, fighting, dreaming, talking, washing dishes, watching TV, it likes to keep going, to spend all its energy. The Jacks of all centers loathe interruptions. On freeways or highways, when someone cuts us off they interrupt the Jacks and this, for the Jacks, is a sin punishable by whatever means are available.

The study of parts of centers helps us understand the way the parts move in us – or rather move us – like parts of a well-oiled machine, without our even being aware of the movement. For example, most of the time when we think we are thinking meaningful thoughts, the thoughts, are really thinking themselves, almost without our participation. They are just riding through our minds on rhythms of association, just passing through our awareness like pedestrians walking through an intersection. In the Jack of Diamonds, where most of our mental activity takes place, quality of though doesn't matter. What's important to the Jack is motion, movement of the thought process. In the Jack we'll be talking, maybe babbling to ourselves, about things we have to do or shouldn't have done; reliving conversations with people long since gone from the scene; imaging conversations we'd like to have; deceiving ourselves about what we really want or need. This kind of thinking – more like endless mental churning – is much different than King of Diamonds thinking, which would inspire a more creative mathematical reasoning, or logic.

Similarly, if we begin to observe our emotional life through this study, we can begin to see how most of our emotions are overwhelmingly repetitive, associative and accidental – in short, are located in the Jack of Hearts. Rarely do we express our emotions with an intellectual intelligence (the King), as in the case of a poet – or even with an emotional intelligence (the Queen), as in the case of a pianist, or a person consciously sorting through his feelings. Rather, emotions run through us with a reason and plan all their own. This is not to say that in ordinary life, one should express emotions as eloquently as a poet or pianist; simply that it is possible to observe the extent to which many of our behavioral manifestations—which we so highly prize – are in fact little more than a general audience playing out their prerecorded likes and dislikes under the banner of our name. By making this observation we open ourselves to new possibilities, we begin to transcend the enslavement of habit.

The Unifier

This center, also known as the Sex Center, cannot be an individual's 'Center of Focus.' The unifier resides equally in each of the four centers – intellectual, emotional, moving, and instinctive. We call it the unifier, because its function is to unify centers, parts of centers, body type, alchemy, chief feature and center of focus. The unifier, represented in the cards by Aces, is like water: we bake with it, drink with it, swim in it, bathe in it, feel it pump through our bodies; it is omnipresent, but often invisible. All four centers use unifier energy. They steal it from each other and from other people, they save it as one would save money in the bank. The unifier is our main energy source.

When we are most ourselves, at "peak" performance, or during a "peak" experience, all four centers work as one. The human race's greatest moments, greatest works of art, highest states of spiritual experience, most important inventions, all come when the four brains are united in purpose. In football, for example, a great quarterback will have the strategic overview of the intellectual center, a sense for the "mood" of the playing field with the emotional center, an ability to dodge those rushing to tackle, which comes from the moving center, and an instinctive sense of when to run and when and where to throw the football.

When we fall in love, all four centers and parts of centers focus on a single point: the object of love. Imagine how much we could accomplish if every moment of our lives were this focused. Usually our body type, alchemy, center of focus and chief feature go out of their way to steal unifier energy from the weaker parts. Fervor, excessiveness, blind faith, jealousy, decadence are all expressions of the abuse of sex energy: unifier energy. And such abuse creates a failure of conscience which in its turn limits our creative and spiritual possibilities. If the unifier worked properly in all human beings crime would cease to exist, waste would vanish, perspective would multiply, spiritual evolution would dominate. An outcome which stands for the moment, somewhat out of reach.

Centers and Preferences

The activities and behavior of the four centers in any given moment are always a result of more than one part governed by center of focus. For example, if an intellectually-centered person writes poetry, for him the poetry begins with a thought in the intellectual center, then a feeling in the emotional center, a sensation in the instinctive center, and a movement in the moving center.

Each center of focus will have its own perception of what is dramatic, exciting, exhilarating, fun to experience. To the intellectually-centered person, the challenge of discovering new ideas will be most dramatic, or trying to complete a mathematical problem, realizing an ultimate formula that nobody else has figured out. For an emotionally-centered person, trying to comprehend some equation is hardly dramatic; it's feelings that count. An intellectually-centered type will tend to respond with an "I think" rather than "I feel." For the moving-centered person, drama will require the expression of moving-centered excellence. The highest pole vault, the perfect design, shape or form, the most graceful dancer, winning the final tennis match, finishing the puzzle. The success of moving-centered skills will be primary.

Our perception overall of violence will depend on which brain dominates in us. So will our perception of what is good, meaningful and valuable. The activities in which we excel are also governed by the dominance of our center of focus. Thus, intellectually-centered people regularly exhibit confidence in intellectual matters – theories, expositions of ideas, and so on. Moving-centered people exhibit confidence in moving-centered activities – sports, crafts, dance. Emotionally-centered people are confident in emotionally-centered activities like social gatherings, weddings, extended periods of trauma, or just being with people. Instinctively-centered people are most sure in instinctively-centered matters like health care, defense of the body, home, and family, security.

What is easiest for an individual to learn largely revolves around his or her center of focus. For example:

MOVING CENTER: Learning to swim, ski, ride, golf, dance, walk, draw.

INSTINCTIVE CENTER: cooking, healing arts, massage, gardening, animal trainer.

INTELLECTUAL CENTER: journalism, law, mathematics, science, academics.

EMOTIONAL CENTER: social etiquette, business relations, negotiator, parenting.

On the whole, men are more intellectually-centered, women are more emotionally-centered. Women will discuss love and relationships from an emotional point-of-view. Men will be mental about the subject. After that, men will be instinctive, and then maybe emotional. Thus, men have a long way to go to understand women, because the emotional center perceives and understands much faster than the intellectual center. Emotions move through us like lightning;thoughts take much longer. First the perception comes; the substance of the emotion; then the image recognition of the emotion follows; and finally, the inner talk that intellectualizes the emotion. (Men generally don't notice an emotion until after the intellectualization begins.) Additionally, we usually have to go through the instinctive center before reaching the emotional center. This is one method the instinctive center employs to protect itself. The emotional center often disregards instinctive limitations; therefore, the instinctive center monitors emotions like a guard at the door of a palace. The instinctive center fears strong emotional experience.

A person will have greater capacity for memory within his dominant center of focus. Thus, an intellectually-centered person will remember numbers easily; a moving-centered person will remember how to do things; emotionally-centered people remember other people. Instinctively-centered people remember tastes and smells.

People in the intellectual center are the most pleasing to watch in intellectually-centered activities, such as chess or a political debate. You'll find them at parties talking about politics or about the latest book they've read. Emotionally-centered people are pleasing to watch in emotionally-centered situations, such as sports commentator, party host, and disk jockey. It is most natural for the emotionally-centered person to be talking with people about people. Moving-centered people are the most pleasing to watch in moving-centered activities, such as sports. You'll see them in tennis tournaments, football games, dance, acrobatics. It's most natural for them to be talking to people about moving-centered activities. You're going to feel the instinctive type could be a chef talking about food and showing people how to cook, or maintain good health and safety.

Our perceptions of pain as well as pleasure are influenced by center of focus. The worst thing for a moving type, for example, is to have movement restricted, forced or eliminated. For the instinctive types, not being allowed to eat or sleep or have sex when they want; restricted sensation, or controlled sensations, horrifies them. For the emotional types, it's terrible to have someone else control who they see. Emotional types need to be free emotionally. They like to be with whom they want when they want. Intellectual types suffer most from having their thought restricted, from having their investigation into ideas restricted.

As with Body Type, Alchemy, and Chief Feature, Center of Focus basically means an imbalance of interest: we focus too much on a part of ourselves, rather than on the whole of ourselves. So someone who is very good at mathematics might be very bad at relationships with people. They can never really be close to people, talking to people is difficult because they're intellectually-centered. Mental activity is primary, and becomes impersonal rather than warm. Emotionally-centered people are very humane, whereas someone with an intellectual center of focus if not in the emotional part of the intellectual center, can appear cold.

And the problem of improving ourselves is not so much one of increased diversification, as it is our inability to know which part to play and when to play it.

Each of the centers of focus has a positive and negative side. This dichotomy is shown in the chart below:

CENTER	POSITIVE	NEGATIVE
Intellectual	Yes	No
Emotional	Feel good	Feel Bad
Moving	Moving	Not Moving
Instinctive	Pleasure/Health	Pain/Disease

We can get another view of center of focus by observing how the different centers relate to other people. Intellectual types want to know what others think. Emotional types want to "feel" what others feel. Moving types want to do what others are doing. Instinctive types want to touch what others are touching (for which reason, instinctively-centered people tend to need sex more than the other centers of focus.)

Religious beliefs also will be affected by center of focus. Religious leaders will create conditions for people to work in that revolve around their own center of focus. For example, an intellectually-centered religious leader will see spirituality in an intellectual framework. Purity of religious doctrine will be framed in terms of ideas, literature, rules, codes of conduct.

Mosaic law is an example of an intellectually-centered religious system, as is the Code of Hummurabi, and our Declaration of Independence and Constitution. Maimonidean Thirteen Articles of Faith, the proofs of God of Thomas Aquinas and the Zen Koans are examples of intellectually-centered religious paradigms. (Compare, for example, the intellectualism of Aquinas with the emotional rawness of St. Augustine in his book, *Confessions*.)

It follows that an intellectually-centered person will be attracted to an intellectually-centered belief system. This person will be disdainful of religious experiences involving intense emotionality, devotionalism, faith, or moving-centered experiences of pilgrimage or dance or, instinctive experiences of body control, fasting, celibacy, sexual revelation. Thus, an emotionally-centered person will follow or teach, or create a religion in which there is emotional harmony, emotional understanding, emotional perception, emotional depth; a religion where there is community, a love of family, a love of God. Communion during Mass can be seen as an emotionally-centered religious experience in which the participant fully experiences the love of God.

A moving-centered person will see spirituality as a result achieved through controlling actions, through monitoring the movement of the organism (the Whirling Dervishes). Tai Chi and yoga draw on the resources of the moving center. Moving-center religions will study and train the way you walk, sit, move. Instinctively-centered leaders will focus on massage, on touching the body, on having spiritually oriented physical experience. Hands on healing is an instinctively-centered phenomenon. Witches, witch doctors, warlocks, the casting of spells and acupuncturists provide an instinctively-centered approach to religion and healing.

Each center will have its own idea of what it needs to feel good about being in the world. For example, intellectually-centered people think as long as they have books, everything is okay. Emotionally-centered people think as long as they are around people, they are all right. Moving-centered people think as long as they can do something it is okay. Instinctively-centered people are often involved in saving the planet, because the planet is sensual and alive. They will be forest rangers, while the intellectually-centered people might be under a tree reading, or in the ranger's office figuring out the financing.

One benefit of this study is that people will learn to spend more time in each of the centers. An intellectually-centered person may give up part of his reading program and learn to enjoy taking a walk. So often, we have a relatively fixed view of life with many perceptions stemming from our center of focus. Someone might say, "it's a waste of time to go to parties; I'd rather stay home and read about the soul." Another person would say, "all books in the world are a waste, unless you're interacting with people." Yet another says, "The best thing to do is to keep moving – writing, running, mowing the lawn, dancing. Someone else thinks: "The only thing that's important is weight-lifting and developing the body." A morality attaches to each position, but this is merely bestowing homage upon the imbalance of our center of focus. Through self-observation, we see our biases and how our dominant center creates a moralistic limited view of the world. We begin to enjoy more, to permit neglected aspects of ourselves to experience life. Also, as with the body type, alchemy and chief feature, our dominant center is followed by a second strongest center. For example, an intellectually-centered type may be good at sports by virtue of a strong moving center; an instinctively-centered person might also be a math prodigy. An emotionally-centered type a good chef. Having this second strength often creates the illusion of a well-rounded and balanced life, and suggests to us that our worldwide view is whole and objective. If only one center of focus were open to us it would be more obvious that our opinions are rather slanted and one dimensional.

Center of Focus and Physical Structure

Like body type and alchemy, center of focus just as definitely affects the appearance of our physical body. For example, emotionally-centered people are often overweight and they remain subject to weight fluctuation throughout their lives. They are soft-skinned people who perspire easily and tend to have more moisture in their skin. Emotionally-centered people are not tight like instinctive or moving types, and their facial features are slightly rounded or pudgy.

Moving types are often well-proportioned or slim, because moving types enjoy the pleasure of physical movement, and any kind of exercise. Intellectual types are classically thin, and their movements are more hesitant, as they often need to think to move. Instinctively-centered people are often stocky, usually strong, with the male having a thicker neck. They are more muscular than fatty. Abundant body hair is also common and they will have slightly larger or flared nostrils and ears.

Tendency Chart #12 – Center of Focus

Person	Body Type	Center of Focus
ARNOLD SCHWARZENGGER	SATURN MARS	MOVING CENTERED JACK OF SPADES
NICKE NOLTE	SATURN MARS	MOVING CENTERED QUEEN OF SPADES
BURT LANCASTER	SATURN MARS	EMOTIONALLY CENTERED JACK OF HEARTS
PRINCESS DIANA	SATURN MARS	EMOTIONALLY CENTERED JACK OF HEARTS
DAN QUAYLE	MARS SOLAR	MOVING CENTERED JACK OF SPADES
PAUL NEWMAN	MARS SOLAR	MOVING CENTERED JACK OF SPADES
BRAD PITT	MARS SOLAR	MOVING CENTERED JACK OF SPADES
ELIZABETH TAYLOR	VENUSIAN MERCURY	EMOTIONALLY CENTERED QUEEN OF HEARTS
BURT REYNOLDS	VENUSIAN MERCURY	INSTINCTIVELY CENTERED QUEEN OF CLUBS
BARBARA HERSHEY	VENUSIAN MERCURY	MOVING CENTERED QUEEN OF SPADES
SYLVESTER STALLONE	VENUSIAN MERCURY	MOVING CENTERED JACK OF SPADES
FRANK SINATRA	VENUSIAN MERCURY	EMOTIONALLY CENTERED QUEEN OF HEARTS
BURT REYNOLDS	VENUSIAN MERCURY	INSTINCTIVELY CENTERED QUEEN OF CLUBS
WARREN BEATTY	VENUSIAN MERCURY	EMOTIONALLY CENTERED JACK OF HEARTS
JAY LENO	VENUSIAN MERCURY	EMOTIONALLY CENTERED JACK OF HEARTS
DUSTIN HOFFMAN	VENUSIAN MERCURY	MOVING CENTERED QUEEN OF SPADES
BARBRA STREISAND	VENUSIAN MERCURY	EMOTIONALLY CENTERED QUEEN OF HEARTS

Continue

Person	Body Type	Center of Focus
JOHN TRAVOLTA	VENUSIAN MERCURY	MOVING CENTERED QUEEN OF SPADES
ROBIN WILLIAMS	VENUSIAN MERCURY	INTELLECTUALLY CENTERED QUEEN OF DIAMONDS
JOHNNY CARSON	MERCURY SOLAR	INTELLECTUALLY CENTERED JACK OF DIAMONDS
EDDIE MURPHY	MERCURY SOLAR	MOVING CENTERED JACK OF SPADES
WHITNEY HOUSTON	MERCURY SOLAR	MOVING CENTERED QUEEN OF SPADES
NICHOLAS CAGE	MERCURY SOLAR	MOVING CENTERED QUEEN OF SPADES
LEONARD NIMOY	MERCURY SATURN	INTELLECTUALLY CENTERED QUEEN OF DIAMONDS
JEFF GOLDBLUM	MERCURY SATURN	MOVING CENTERED QUEEN OF SPADES
RAJIV GANDHI	LUNAR VENUSIAN	EMOTIONALLY CENTERED JACK OF HEARTS
SIDNEY POITIER	SOLAR SATURN	EMOTIONALLY CENTERED KING OF HEARTS
DALAI LAMA	JOVIAL LUNAR	EMOTIONALLY CENTERED KING OF HEARTS
GOLDIE HAWN	SOLAR LUNAR	MOVING CENTERED QUEEN OF SPADES
QUEEN ELIZABETH II	LUNAR	INSTINCTIVELY CENTERED QUEEN OF CLUBS
HILLARY CLINTON	MARS	EMOTIONALLY CENTERED JACK OF HEARTS
MARGARET THATCHER	MARS	INSTINCTIVELY CENTERED QUEEN OF CLUBS
DEMI MOORE	MERCURY SATURN	EMOTIONALLY CENTERED JACK OF HEARTS
CANDACE BERGEN	SATURN MARS	INSTINCTIVELY CENTERED JACK OF CLUBS
BARBARA WALTERS x	MARS	INTELLECTUALLY CENTERED JACK OF DIAMONDS

Continue

Person	Body Type	Center of Focus
BILL CLINTON	VENUSIAN MERCURY	EMOTIONALLY CENTERED JACK OF HEARTS
RICHARD NIXON	VENUSIAN MERCURY	INTELLECTUALLY CENTERED QUEEN OF DIAMONDS
GEORGE BUSH	LUNAR	INTELLECTUALLY CENTERED JACK OF DIAMONDS
SADDAM HUSSEIN	VENUSIAN MERCURY	EMOTIONALLY CENTERED QUEEN OF HEARTS
HITLER	VENUSIAN MERCURY	MOVING CENTERED QUEEN OF SPADES
JOHN MAJOR	LUNAR	INSTINCTIVELY CENTERED JACK OF DIAMONDS
BORIS YELTSIN	MARS JOVIAL	EMOTIONALLY CENTERED QUEEN OF HEARTS

Tendency Chart #13 – Center of Focus

Center of Focus	Other Examples
INTELLECTUAL	EINSTEIN, MR. SPOCK, CHESS, BRIDGE, MATH MAJANG, ENGLAND, SCOTLAND, AUSTRIA, JAPAN
EMOTIONAL	ELIZABETH TAYLOR, JOHN CANDY ITALY, SPAIN, INDONESIA BEAR, ST. BERNARD, GORILLA
INSTINCTIVE	CLINT EASTWOOD, CHARLES BRONSON GREECE , RUSSIA, GERMANY CROCODILE, HAWK, SKUNK
MOVING	GLENDA JACKSON, PATRICK SWAYZE TURKEY, SCANDINAVIA, USA, FRANCE, AUSTRALIA MONKEY, CAT, DEER, GISELLE, GREYHOUND, CHITA

Tendency Chart #14 – Center of Focus
Deck of Cards Diagram

Suits and their relationship to the four centers of focus

CLUBS	SPADES	HEARTS	DIAMONDS
INSTINCTIVE CENTER	MOVING CENTER	EMOTIONAL CENTER	INTELLECTUAL CENTER

KINGS	QUEENS	JACKS
10	7	4
9	6	3
8	5	2

ACE IN EACH SUIT represents "The Unifier"

JOKERS represent higher emotional & intellectual centers; the two higher states of consciousness.

The Suit of Diamonds

King   The King of Diamonds represents the intellectual part of the intellectual center.

10   Within the King, the ten of diamonds represents the intellectual part of the intellectual part of the intellectual center.

9   The nine of diamonds represents the Emotional part of the Intellectual part of the Intellectual center.

8   The eight of diamonds represents the Moving or Instinctive part of the Intellectual part of the intellectual center.

Queen   The queen of diamonds represents the Emotional part of the Intellectual center

7   Within the queen, the seven of diamonds represents the Intellectual part of the Emotional part of the Intellectual center.

6   The six of diamonds represents the Emotional part of the Emotional part of the Intellectual center.

5   The five of diamonds represents the Moving or Instinctive part of the Emotional part of the Intellectual center.

Jack   The jack of diamonds represents the Moving or Instinctive part of the Intellectual center.

4   Within the jack, the four of diamonds represents the Intellectual part of the Moving or Instinctive part of the Intellectual center.

3   The three of diamonds represents the Emotional part of the Moving or Instinctive part of the intellectual center.

2   The two of diamonds represents the Moving or Instinctive part of the Moving or Instinctive part of the Intellectual center.

The Suit of Hearts

King   The king of hearts represents the Intellectual part of the Emotional Center

10   Within the king, the ten of hearts represents the Intellectual part of the Intellectual part of the Emotional center.

9   The nine of hearts represents the Emotional part of the Intellectual part of the Emotional center.

8   The eight of hearts represents the Moving or Instinctive part of the Intellectual part of the Emotional center.

Queen   The queen of hearts represents the Emotional part of the Emotional center.

7   Within the queen, the seven of hearts represents the Intellectual part of the Emotional part of the Emotional center.

6   The six of hearts represents the Emotional part of the Emotional part of the Emotional center.

5   The five of hearts represents the Moving or Instinctive part of the Emotional part of the Emotional center.

Jack   The jack of hearts represents the Moving or Instinctive part of the Emotional center.

4   Within the jack, the four of hearts represents the Intellectual part of the Moving or Instinctive part of the Emotional center.

3   The three of hearts represents the Emotional part of the Moving or Instinctive part of the Emotional center.

2   The two of hearts represents the Moving or Instinctive part of the Moving or Instinctive part of the Emotional center.

The Suit of Spades

King   The king of spades represents the Intellectual part of the Moving center.

10   Within the king, the ten of spades represents the Intellectual part of the Intellectual part of the Moving center.

9   The nine of spades represents the Emotional part of the Intellectual part of the Moving center.

8   The eight of spades represents the Moving or Instinctive part of the Intellectual part of the Moving center.

Queen   The queen of spades represents the Emotional part of the Moving center.

7   Within the queen, the seven of spades represents the Intellectual part of the Emotional part of the Moving center.

6   The six of spades represents the Emotional part of the Emotional part of the Moving center.

5   The five of spades represents the Moving or Instinctive part of the Emotional part of the Moving center

Jack   The jack of spades represents the Moving or Instinctive part of the Moving center.

4   Within the jack, the four of spades represents the Intellectual part of the Moving or Instinctive part of the Moving center.

3   The three of spades represents the Emotional part of the Moving or Instinctive part of the Moving center.

2   The two of spades represents the Moving or Instinctive part of the Moving or Instinctive part of the Moving center.

The Suit of Clubs

King   The king of clubs represents the Intellectual part of the Instinctive center

10   Within the king, the ten of clubs represents the Intellectual part of the Intellectual part of the Instinctive center.

9   The nine of clubs represents the Emotional part of the Intellectual part of the Instinctive center.

8   The eight of clubs represents the Moving or Instinctive part of the Intellectual part of the Instinctive center.

Queen   The queen of clubs represents the Emotional part of the Instinctive center.

7	Within the queen, the seven of clubs represents the Intellectual part of the Emotional part of the Instinctive center.
6	The six of clubs represents the Emotional part of the Emotional part of the Instinctive center.
5	The five of clubs represents the Moving or Instinctive part of the Emotional part of the Instinctive center.
Jack	The jack of clubs represents the Moving or Instinctive part of the Instinctive center.
4	Within the jack, the four of clubs represents the Intellectual part of the Moving or Instinctive part of the Instinctive center.
3	The three of clubs represents the Emotional part of the Moving or Instinctive part of the Instinctive center.
2	The two of clubs represents the Moving or Instinctive part of the Moving or Instinctive part of the Instinctive center.

Essence

Essence and Personality

Essence is perhaps the most complex feature of a human being. Many of our foibles, talents and quirks originate in essence. Essence is the non-categorical side of human behavior, the illogical side. Essence is what we are as an individual, the one thing that ensures us of occupying a wholly unique position in the flood of creation. In short, type, feature, alchemy, and center of focus are what all humans have in common, what we have been given rather than what we have earned; that which makes the "masses," the masses. Essence is what makes the individual, individual. In theory, essence is that accumulated experience arisen in us from the soil of past lives, what Hindus call Karma.

Essence is the home of belief: that side of the human nature which is our greatest commodity. To control an individual's belief system is to control his source of conscience, his most essential life force. All governments, religions, organizations, corporations and causes seek to influence and subjugate Essence and our belief system; to advance in us their beliefs which transform into our false personality.

Foundation Knowledge draws an important distinction between essence and false personality. False personality is comprised largely of a person's opinions and learned or acquired beliefs, which can change in a matter of minutes through peer pressure, persuasion, new information, difficult circumstances, or hypnosis. It's rather shocking to realize that

men of conviction often stand in shallow water. With receipt
of a million dollars, what we tend to regard as essential can
vanish. This will not happen with essence. Essence is solid
to actually change it requires more pressure than most people
can live through. Personality does not change Essence, it
buries Essence.

Personality itself is divided into false personality and true
personality. Our false personality is made of what others have
told us to think, feel, and do, what others have said is right or
wrong. False personality includes opinions and beliefs which
are not our own, not representative of our own true feelings
and yet taken to be our own. These opinions and beliefs give
us a sense of certainty, a sense of being in control, especially
when they originate from someone we admire, trust or respect.
The feelings of 'I like" or "I don't like" can be powerful tool
for believing we are in charge of our destiny. But we are not
in charge. By studying foundation knowledge, what we can
and cannot control, what is and is not real, what we are and
what we are not, becomes more clear. We become at least a
little more objective, and begin to have more choice. This is
where true personality can develop. True personality represents those opinions, attitudes and feelings we have about our
selves, other people and life in general which are based on the
acquisition of self-knowledge, objective conscience and the
establishment of multi-dimensional perspective. And true
personality, in its mature stage, protects essence and provides
for the birth of the immortality of essence: freedom from the
lower laws of the third dimension.

Essence and Being

In Essence we find the "state" of our being. To be good-
hearted, kind, revengeful, hateful, suspicious, angry, jealous
lustful, forgiving, is to be in a 'state' of being which reflects

qualities of an individual's essence. There are 'good' and 'evil' essences. Being is what a person is, and Essence is the state of that being. The state of Essence can move toward developing greater being or developing powers. Choice is in essence. When choice is decided and we are just reacting, as in the cases where we are influenced by a strong external force, body type, chief feature, center of focus, etc., essence is omitted while we are children. Essence is more elastic and capable of change. One could say it is undecided. It functions with a very fine hydrogen (Hydrogen 24.) This provides much more opportunity to evolve one's identity from a one dimensional perspective to a multi-dimensional perspective. Body type, center of focus, alchemy, and chief feature function with a heavier hydrogen. The difference of moving your hand through air vs moving it through sand can best describe relationships of lighter versus heavier hydrogen applications. Moving one's hand through air would exemplify Hydrogen 24 (Essence) as opposed to moving it through sand or cement (Body Type, Chief feature, etc.).

While essence, (as a state rather than a function), is distinct from the more mechanical functions of body type, chief feature, alchemy and center of focus, essence influences and is influenced by these functions. For example, if your essence is good-hearted, but you are a negative body type, you'll tend to be more tolerant in negative situations. Similarly, if your essence is jealous and angry, and you are a negative body type, you'll use the type to express your state of anger – you'll destroy, or cheat your adversary with little or no remorse.

When body type, chief feature, center of focus and alchemy are controlled by other people they influence essence too much and we tend to live more in a personality which is false, or untrue to essence – that is, a false personality. For example, if you are living in a city where the ideal of beauty is the tall, sleek and firm Saturn-Mars woman, and you are, in essence, a lazy and affectionate type who prefers eating to jogging, the culture – which in this example is controlled by body type – will lead you into a state of mind which demands that you be other than what you are. You begin to jog and exercise everyday, learn to loathe your soft and "weak" body; you do all you can to change. You become a Saturn-Mars in body and spirit, even though your essence is more in harmony with the Venusian type. The culture tells you your essence is unacceptable; so you put on a false personality, which eventually buries your essence.

If outside pressure from parents, schools, governments and peers forces us to adopt a type or behavioral mode which is not our own, essence is affected even defeated.

The principles of body type, alchemy, feature and center of focus are functions, tools, whose use reflects the state of our being; the degree to which we are not "ourselves." When essence controls type, we are more individual, less false; on the other hand, if essence is ruled by type and externals, we are less of an individual. The objective is to observe these influences and how they affect us, and by observation, to free ourselves from them, so that we can live more in essence and less in false personality.

Essence and Spirituality

Essence is a very complex embodiment of related differences from which many systems of behavioral control and categorization are developed. For example, in Freudian Psychology; there was something in Freud's essence that provided him with the framework for psychotherapy today; which is not an objective system of behavioral evaluation. Many offshoot religious practices are based on an essence perception of what is good for an individual. And that individual convinces other people that what is good for him is good for them. Essence is not objective. It's wonderful, but it's still not objective.

• • •

Study of Foundation Knowledge helps to reduce the belief that our survival depends upon overcoming and condemning others for expressing the given tendencies of their body type, alchemy, chief feature and center of focus. With an increase in understanding we reduce the misuse of our critical faculty. This renders us less judgmental toward ourselves, other people, and toward the world around us, especially toward circumstances we cannot control.

If, for example, you know a person's body type, and understand that possible causes for certain tendencies are unknown to him, you may develop a less vehement criticism toward his manifestations. Foundation knowledge works as a railman's sledgehammer, breaking the chain of our habitual and generally thoughtless reactions, with knowledge the choice is ours, and choice provides a greater opportunity for spiritual growth.

One underlying theme of this book is to illustrate how often we react rather then act, and that our existence is too often little more than a series of indifferent one dimensional responses to various stimuli. Most of these responses are typical, if not archetypal. The greater our recognition of how we are stimulated, the greater our ability to choose a response.

The highest application of foundation knowledge comes when "I", the human concept of individual human identity or ego, rises above its attachment to the subject of observation to become the state of observation itself. The more we know about body type, alchemy, chief feature and center of focus, the more we know ourselves; the more we know what is not spirit. Much of what we believe to be divine are laws; multiple aspects of the diverse and complex factors which make humans, human. To become more spiritually evolved first implies that we become more human, to become more aware of what we are, as human, not to change what we are. If we can verify and utilize the knowledge of body type, alchemy, chief feature and center of focus, the differences between those tendencies which are given and those which are earned will become clear to us. And clarity is our best teacher.

Tendency Chart #15 – Essence

Influences which act positively upon essence

Individual	Heredity	National
SINGING	FORESTRY	FRENCH
WRITING	BLACKSMITH	GERMAN
DESIGNING	THE ARTS	SPANISH
SYMPATHETIC	MEDICINE	ENGLISH
COOKING	RELIGION	DUTCH
VISIONARY	LAW ENFORCEMENT	SOUTH AMERICA
PATIENCE	HOSPITALITY	AFRICAN
HUMOR	ENTERTAINMENT	AUSTRALIAN
FAITHFULNESS	JOURNALISM	RUSSIAN
INTUITIVENESS	CUISINE	CHINESE
COMPASSION	MILITARY	INDIAN
LOVE	TECHNOLOGY	BRAZILIAN
Individual natural tendencies & abilities	Family Background	Ethnic & Cultural Background

Tendency Chart #16– Essence
Influences which act negatively upon essence

Individual	Heredity
HATE	MERCENARY
BITTERNESS	EXECUTIONERS
BIGOTRY	CLEPTOMANIA
SATANISM	SCHIZOPHRENIA
RUTHLESSNESS	MULTIPLE SCLEROSIS
PHOBIAS	POLIO
SADOMASOCHISM	ALZHEIMER'S
HEDONISM	MOLESTERS
LUST	RAPISTS
CRUELTY	MURDERS
SUICIDAL	ALCOHOLISM
NERVOUS DISORDERS	DRUG ABUSE

Recommended reading

The following is a list of recommended reading material for the student who desires a greater understanding of the back ground of this system of typology, or who would like to look into other systems of typology.

Gurdjieff & Ouspensky Teachings:

The foundations of the material presented in this book are derived from the system of G. I. Gurdjieff, an early 20th century mystic-philosopher-trickster-cosmologist. For a deeper understanding of the principles of Foundation Knowledge the following books are recommended.

* Ouspensky, P. D.; "In Search of the Miraculous."
The most interesting and readable presentation of the Gurdjieffian system of knowledge, in its entirety, presented with the backdrop of the Russian revolution.

* Collin, Rodney; "The Theory of Celestial Influence."
Another highly readable and fascinating study of the Gurdjieff system with explanations of the eneagram, and further elaborations of typology, cosmology and sociology.

* Nicoll, Maurice; "Psychological Commentaries on the Teachings of Gurdjieff and Ouspensky," 5 Vols.
A superb and detailed analysis of the Gurdjieffian system from a psychological perspective.

* Friedlander, Joel; "Body Types," first published in 1986. A very clear and precise rendition of body type knowledge.

* Sheldrake, Rubert; "New Science of Life."

Other Typological Systems:

There have been many typological systems developed throughout the millennium originating in different cultures and developed by different teachers. All of these systems will give the student further insights into the nature of human psychology. We give here a list of several of the more common systems and several titles to direct the student in his search for further information.

Astrology:

For a study of western astrology we recommend the works of Sepharial and Alan Leo as excellent introductions to the field. See below for further details on finding specific titles.

In the field of eastern astrology, the following titles are recommended:

* Frawley, David; "The Astrology of the Seers: A Guide to Vedic (Hindu) Astrology."
This is an excellent introduction to eastern astrology.

* Braha, James T.; "Ancient Hindu Astrology for the Modern Western Astrologer."
This excellent books helps to bridge the gap between eastern and western astrology.

Numerology:

There are a large number of books available on numerology, again see below, but here are a few to get started.

* Sepharial; "The Kabala of Numbers."
* Montrose; "Numerology for Everybody."
* Taylor, Ariel Yvon; "Numerology Made Plain."
* Balliet, Mrs. L. Dow; "The Philosophy of Numbers."

Tarot:

Again there are many books available on the tarot but we consider the following to be excellent.
* Papus; "The Tarot of the Bohemians."

Psychology and Mythology:

There are a number of more recent typological systems based upon both psychological and mythological components. As an exploration of this field we suggest the following.

* Campbell, Joseph; "The Hero With a Thousand Faces."
Joseph Campbell has done an excellent job correlating mythology with life, and hence mythic characters and stories with psychological types and life experiences.

* Bolen, Jean Shinoda; "Gods in Everyman and also Goddesses in Everywoman." A template correlating the archetypes of mythic gods and goddesses with human types.

* Myers-Briggs *Personality Evaluation*. This is a psychological test and evaluation given by psychologists which interestingly distinguishes typological characteristics of individuals.

For information on further typological systems and for more detailed information on the systems listed above, or to attain many of the above listed books, please contact the Sacred Science Institute at (800) 756-6141 or on the Internet a www.sacredscience.com.

W. Bradstreet Stewart, Founder of the Sacred Science Institute (www.sacredscience.com), a unique Internet resource promoting research and development in the field of esoteric cosmology.

Notes

Notes

Notes

Notes

Notes